Cain's
The Story of Liverpool in a Pint

Cain's

The Story of Liverpool
in a Pint

Christopher Routledge

Liverpool University Press

First published 2008
Liverpool University Press
4 Cambridge Street
Liverpool, L69 7ZU

British Library Cataloguing-in-Publication Data
A British Library CIP Record is available.

ISBN 978-1-84631-150-5

Set in Berling Nova by
Koinonia, Manchester
Printed in the European Union by
Bell and Bain Ltd, Glasgow

Printed and bound by CPI Group (UK) Ltd, Croydon, CR0 4YY

Contents

Acknowledgements

The research for this book was greatly assisted by appeals for information in the *Liverpool Echo*, the *Daily Post*, and on Claire Hamilton's show on BBC Radio Merseyside. The people of Liverpool responded with characteristic enthusiasm and generosity. Anita Carlisle, Charles Taylor and Helen Webb deserve special thanks for allowing me to see documents and other material from their family archives. At the brewery, Ajmail and Sudarghara Dusanj were very generous with their time and with their support. At Liverpool University Press I wish to thank Simon Bell who had the idea for this book in the first place and Anthony Cond for his encouragement at every stage. It's been a pleasure working with them.

Preface: Liverpool in a Pint

This book tells the story of Cain's brewery in Liverpool, a story of success, failure and rebirth. Cain's is a classic 'rags to riches' immigrant story. A young Irishman, fresh from a spell at sea, entered the brewing trade and by his own skill, hard work and ability managed to take advantage of the local market. By the time of his death sixty years later his company was one of the largest regional breweries in Britain and one of the largest companies of any kind in Edwardian England. He was the owner of a huge and ornate mansion, and the proprietor of a state-of-the-art brewery as well as over 200 pubs. He died in 1907, Liverpool's 700th anniversary year, when the city and his brewery were at the height of their success. The brewery changed hands several times during the twentieth century and faced closure more than once. Then, in a twist that brings the brewery and the city full circle, it was bought by two brothers, Ajmail and Sudarghara Dusanj, the sons of an immigrant from the Punjab. Thus, this is also the story of two immigrant families separated by continents, by culture, and by the long stretch of one hundred and fifty years.

Brewing is one of the oldest human activities and one of

the most important. It is found almost everywhere, across thousands of years of history, and across continents. From the moment it was first discovered that cereal grains could be fermented to make beer, people have worked on the brewing process to make distinctive, good-quality ales. Like football teams, breweries and beer are part of the identity of many regions. Who could think of Newcastle without Brown Ale, Dublin without Guinness, or London without its Pride? Where else but Scotland could you ask for a pint of Heavy and be understood?

The story of Cain's, like the story of Liverpool, is one of passion, ambition and graft. It takes in immigration, global trade, terrible poverty and vast wealth. In just two generations the Cain family went from the slums of Irish Liverpool to a seat in the House of Lords. As the city grew so did the brewery, and as it struggled, so Cain's redbrick 'terracotta palace' fought for its survival.

The remarkable revival of Cain's in the twenty-first century was matched by the city's own reinvention and recovery after decades of neglect and scorn. As shiny glass towers rose over the city centre, Cain's became a flagship for the whole city. Its owners, Ajmail and Sudarghara Dusanj, were local heroes. The company's near-collapse and rescue in the middle of Liverpool's year as European Capital of Culture can be taken as a reminder that second chances, if they come at all, do not come easily.

Here, then, is the story of Liverpool in a pint.

1

An Immigrant Story

The Robert Cain brewery stands on Stanhope Street in Liverpool, not far from the Coburg Dock and the River Mersey. Stanhope Street is an unassuming place in an area of light industrial units, backstreet garages, disused Victorian warehouses, run-down corner pubs and a few terraced houses. In 1858, when Robert Cain acquired the site, it was on the edge of Liverpool's warehousing district, just up the hill from the river and the docks, and surrounded by overcrowded and unhealthy 'court' housing typical of Liverpool's slum areas. The brewery is a remarkable building, rightly considered one of Liverpool's finest. With its ornate terracotta tiles and brickwork, the elaborate crest, the tower and the pretty Brewery Tap pub nestling in one corner, it is a monument to the optimism of Victorian Liverpool.

Work began on the current brewery building in 1887, the year of Queen Victoria's Golden Jubilee. By then Robert Cain was living in a large house not far from Sefton Park, which had opened to the public in 1872. It was one of the newest and most exclusive neighbourhoods in the city. Cain, his wife Ann and the six children then living with them – they had 11 children in all – were tended to by servants. Their home, 'Barn Hey', was on Aigburth Road near to where it joined Lark Lane, and stood in three acres of land. It was one of the grandest houses in an area known for its grand Victorian villas.

The Cains lived a life of comfort and privilege. No doubt the family enjoyed walking in the park when the weather was good, or took boat trips on the lake. Cain's sphere of influence included not only other industrialists, but city councillors and high-status members of Liverpool's Tory elite. Though he never stood for office, Cain, along with several other brewers, was an influential figure behind the scenes in the powerful Conservative Constitutional Association. He collected paintings and rare plants and was every inch the Victorian self-made man.

The story of Robert Cain and his brewery is partly obscured by the 'Cain myths', no doubt authored at first by the man himself and later passed down until they settled as accepted facts in the story of Liverpool. Most problematic of all is the story of his move from Ireland. The best-known version of the rags to riches story begins in 1844 with Cain's arrival in Liverpool as a young man after a period at sea. In this account Cain is an ambitious Irish immigrant coming to Liverpool as part of the great wave of migration that peaked in the famine year of 1847. Pulling himself up by his bootstraps, Cain became an example of what could be achieved through hard work and perseverance. In another variation of the tale, Cain marries the daughter of the Mayor of Liverpool and builds his brewing company on inherited wealth. Still another version gives him a background in the Irish gentry as the son of Mary Deane, whose father was a prominent architect and whose brother became the Mayor of Cork. However, Robert Cain did not arrive in Liverpool in 1844 as a swashbuckling young man of 18. He moved there from County Cork in the 1820s as a small child and grew up an 'Irish slummy' in the Scotland Road ghetto.

Whatever the reasons behind the emergence of the 'authorised' 1844 arrival story, the key to Robert Cain's early life is his father, James Cain, who died from bronchitis in Liverpool on 26 December 1871. James Cain served as a private soldier in the 88th Regiment of Foot, known as the Connaught Rangers, and according to private research commissioned in the 1980s he was the only man of that name to do so. Reference sources as respectable as *Debrett's*, which maintains and researches the genealogical record of the British aristocracy, claim that James Cain was descended from the Ancient Kings of Ulster and that he was a veteran of the Peninsular Wars, which ended in the defeat of Napoleon in 1814.

Although his death certificate claims that he was born in 1786, according to army records James Cain was born in Donaghmoyne, near the town of Carrickmacross, County Monaghan, a decade later in 1796. Perhaps his son-in-law, Pierce Reddy, who was present at his death and witnessed the signing of the certificate, made a mistake or guessed at his age. James Cain grew up in poverty as the Industrial Revolution was getting underway in England, at a time when Ireland was firmly under British control. The failed 1798 revolution brought thousands of British troops into the country to control the population by force, and for most of the nineteenth century between 20,000 and 30,000 British troops were stationed in Ireland. As a young man, James worked as an itinerant labourer before enlisting for life with the '88th Foot' at Chester on 1 December 1820, six years after the Peninsular Wars had ended. There is no record of where he served, but it is almost certain that he was based at the fortified garrison on Spike Island, which the British used to defend the entrance to Cork harbour.

According to the official history of Robert Cain and his family, James Cain married Mary Deane in 1824. Mary Deane was the daughter of Alexander Deane, an Irish architect, and the sister of Sir Thomas Deane, an architect and Mayor of Cork. Yet here, too, there are discrepancies in the story. In 1824 James's wife Mary already had a three-year-old daughter, Hannah. And when Robert Cain's younger brother William was born in Liverpool in 1839, his mother's maiden name was recorded as 'Kirk' in the register of births.

Mary Cain gave birth to her first son, Robert, on 29 April 1826 in the parish of Templerobin on Spike Island, just across a busy shipping lane from the port of Cobh (pronounced 'cove'). By the 1840s, when Robert Cain began brewing in Liverpool, Cobh was one of the most important ports of departure for Irish refugees heading for the United States, Australia and elsewhere. Cobh was renamed Queenstown in 1849 after a visit by Queen Victoria and it became a stopping-off point for ocean liners crossing the Atlantic between Liverpool and the east coast of America. In 1912 the port was the final landfall for *Titanic* before she set off northwards into Arctic waters.

Life in a garrison town could not have been easy, but at a time of high unemployment the Cain family at least had a regular income. James Cain's record as a soldier was good and, aged 30 and in good health, he had several years of active military service ahead of him. But not long after the birth of his son, James Cain suffered an injury that would end his army career and leave him and his young family in poverty. The handwriting on the medical officer's discharge report is unclear, but it appears to describe a chronic shoulder injury with damage to the front and back and stiffness in the joint, possibly consistent with a gunshot wound. Being illiterate and unable to sign his name, James Cain left only his mark on his army discharge papers. Identity theft was common, so as a means to 'prevent any improper use being made of this discharge' the document describes his appearance. On 10 November 1827 James Cain was 'about 31 Years of age, is 5 feet 7 Inches [170cm] in height, fair Hair, grey Eyes, fair Complexion, and by Trade or Occupation a Labourer'. The brewer Robert Cain would later attribute his success in business in part to his physical strength and stamina. Images of him show a man with a powerful neck and barrel chest, and it is not difficult to imagine that he inherited these character-istics from his soldier father.

Ireland in the 1820s was a difficult place to make a living, more so if you were illiterate, unskilled and carrying an injury that made you unfit for active military duty. By then, when crop failures began to hint at the future horrors of the famine of the 1840s, the Irish economy was completely dependent on England. For ordinary people this meant that in times of trouble it was England, not Ireland, that offered the promise of work and the ability to feed their families. In 1827 the United States lifted restrictions on immigration from Britain and James and Mary may have been tempted to join the swelling ranks of Irish heading across the Atlantic. But perhaps because James had already spent time in Liver-pool, or because his wife was pregnant with Robert's younger sister Mary, they settled in the heart of the town's growing Irish ghetto of the North End.

In later life Robert Cain admitted, perhaps even relished, his humble background, but made little of it. The reality is that Cain grew up in the slums where the drinking water was dirty and in short supply, and where many thousands of people crammed into filthy, damp cellars and courts with open sewers running past their doors. Irish Liverpool in the early nineteenth century was a place rife with disease, violence and drunkenness, where high unemployment meant that children and adults went hungry for days at a time. When work could be had it was often dangerous and badly paid. Labourers were hired on a day-to-day basis and were obliged to gather on the dockside every morning to be chosen for work. As the situation in Ireland worsened and increasing numbers of people landed at the quay they were preyed upon by gangs of thieves and conmen who took what little money they had and disappeared. By the 1840s people were actually starving to death on the streets.

This was the world into which James Cain brought his young family and in which they managed to eke out a living. They arrived at the end of 1827 or early in 1828, and by the time of the census in 1841 they were living in Hough Court, off Bent Street in the Islington area of Liverpool. It was a well-known slum and seven people shared the cramped dwelling. Apart from James, Mary and their son Robert, another daughter, Mary, had been born in Liverpool in 1828 and another son, William, was just two years old. By this time Hannah was married and she and her husband, Pierce Reddy, also lived with the family.

After the death of his wife Mary in 1864, James Cain

moved in with the Reddy family, which included his grandson James, who seems to have been a favourite. At the time of the the 1871 census, which was taken on 2 April, the family lived in a court off Holly Street and consisted of seven people, including four of Pierce and Hannah's children: Robert, aged 24, James, aged 16, Ellen, aged nine, and Hannah, aged six. The Reddy family were shoemakers, and apart from a few years in Ireland, where James Reddy was born, they had lived in various court type dwellings in the slums around Scotland Road for most of their lives. Soon after the census, however, they moved round the corner to a more modern tenement at 95 Christian Street. This is where James Cain died. The death certificate records him as a 'pensioner of the 88th Foot'.

Young men growing up in the slums of Liverpool in the early nineteenth century had few choices when it came to the kind of work they did. The docks provided employment for large numbers of labourers and stevedores, while ship-building, ship supplies and warehousing were other possibilities. Poor families could also apprentice or indenture their sons to employers and sometimes received money in return. If they were lucky, as Cain was, they would learn a trade such as coopering, but apprentices were often exploited as cheap labour. Robert Cain's seafaring career began in his teens and was centred on the palm oil shipping routes along the West African coast. It is likely that he was apprenticed to a cooper on board ship. These were among the most unpleasant and dangerous sea voyages of all. The tropical heat, hostile local populations and the threat of malaria earned the whole area a reputation as the 'white man's graveyard'. After several years enduring these difficult conditions, by the mid-1840s

Cain was no doubt ready for a change. He may also have felt resentful towards his father for forcing him into such a dangerous occupation.

Forty years later, when he was featured in the *Liverpool Review* as one of Liverpool's most celebrated sons, Cain used the opportunity to make sure that readers knew he had achieved success through nothing but his own physical, mental and moral strength. No doubt taking a cue from Cain himself, the author of the interview noted that 'If Mr. Cain had begun in the army he would probably have ended being a general'.[1] By then Cain's father was long dead, yet this comment seems to be aimed at him and his failure either to progress in the army or to escape Liverpool's dismal slums. Even at the age of 61 the son had points to score off the father.

Cain's return to Liverpool in the 1840s may account for the story in which 1844 is given as the year of his arrival. Aged 21 he would by then have been free of any obligation to his employer. He almost certainly had plans for starting his own brewing business. Whatever his reasons for staying ashore, the Liverpool to which he returned was a town of sharp contrasts and contradictions.

Liverpool was on the way to becoming known as the 'Gateway of Empire', and while its economic peak was still a long way off, it already had a strong claim to being Britain's second city. Thousands of ships passed through the port. Coasters brought people and cargo from Scotland, Wales, Ireland and other parts of England, while Liverpool ships carried cargoes to and from North America, India, Africa and all points in between. Sailors and passengers from around

1 *Liverpool Review*, 17 September 1887, p. 10.

the world made Liverpool their temporary home in between voyages while overseas trade meant that many native Liverpudlians had experience of life in other countries. But the other side of life in Liverpool was less romantic. The city had already acquired the nickname 'the black spot on the Mersey', for its overcrowding, disease and high death rate. In 1844 there was already a large Irish population, most of whom lived in terrible poverty. As the Irish famine took hold around 1847, Liverpool's Irish ghetto grew exponentially, bringing the city to the brink of conflict and collapse.

Irish immigration to Liverpool came about partly because many ships heading to the United States sailed from there. In *The End of Hidden Ireland*, Robert Scally points out that 'At least two of every three emigrants from Ireland during the 1830s and 1840s passed through Liverpool ... to that number were added the bulk of Scots, Welsh, and English migrants'.[2] The city also had attractions of its own, in particular the promise of work in shipbuilding or one of the many industries that had sprung up to service the port. This meant that even before the famine years of 1847–1849 Liverpool was vastly overpopulated. The number of residents in the city rose from 165,000 to 286,000 in the 1830s alone. By 1840 the large number of men looking for work meant that finding a job was extremely difficult. And with a vast oversupply of labour, rates of pay fell drastically. This was one reason why many migrants never moved on from Liverpool: they simply failed to raise the money for their onward journey.

By 1844 over half a million Irish-born people lived in mainland Britain, mostly in London, Manchester, Liverpool

2 Robert Scally, *The End of Hidden Ireland* (Oxford: Oxford University Press, 1995), p. 184.

and Glasgow. For most of them living conditions were terrible, and in the 1840s Cain would have been familiar with the kind of dwelling described by Frederick Engels in his book *The Condition of the Working Class in England*:

> It often happens that a whole Irish family is crowded into one bed; often a heap of filthy straw or quilts of old sacking cover all in an indiscriminate heap, where all alike are degraded by want, stolidity, and wretchedness. Often the inspectors found, in a single house, two families in two rooms. All slept in one, and used the other as a kitchen and dining-room in common. Often more than one family lived in a single damp cellar, in whose pestilent atmosphere twelve to sixteen persons were crowded together. To these and other sources of disease must be added that pigs were kept, and other disgusting things of the most revolting kind were found.[3]

Engels was writing about Manchester, where 'Little Ireland' covered a small area of the city. In Liverpool conditions were a lot worse and on a much larger scale. For one thing, the city's population grew more quickly. From being smaller than Manchester in 1831 by some 20,000 people, Liverpool's population grew by over 200,000 in the following two decades, reaching 376,000 in 1851 and exceeding Manchester by 73,000 people. The majority of the city's inhabitants were poor, many to the point of starvation.

Part of the problem was that Liverpool's entire population was packed into a relatively small area. In 1845 the built-up area extended not quite as far as Princes Park to the south and east, and to the Canada Dock in the north. Limekiln Lane, where Cain established his first brewery in 1850, ended in open countryside. Walton was a small village

3 Frederick Engels, *The Condition of the Working-Class in England in 1844*. With a Preface Written in 1892 (London: George Allen and Unwin, 1943), pp. 64–65.

and Bootle was just fields; most of the area around Everton
and Anfield had yet to be developed.

While Liverpool's reputation as 'the black spot on the
Mersey' was well deserved, the other side of the city's expansion was wealth and opportunity. Liverpool was a dynamic,
influential place at the leading edge of Britain's economic
growth. In the midst of the chaos fortunes were being made
and a revolution was taking place. The major Victorian
buildings such as the Walker Art Gallery, the City Library
and the museum had yet to be built, but evidence of Liverpool's vitality was plain to see. The first passenger railway
in the world, the Liverpool to Manchester Railway, had
opened in 1830 and by 1840, as 'railway mania' took hold, the
city was linked to Southport, Preston and elsewhere by rail.
By the late 1830s the dock system was among the largest and
most technically advanced anywhere in the world, so much
so in fact that Herman Melville, the American author of
Moby Dick, thought Liverpool's docks far superior to New
York's and was impressed enough to compare them with
the Great Wall of China. Thus, despite the poverty, desti-
tution and disease that were a daily sight on Liverpool's
streets, 1844 was in many ways a good time to settle there.
Especially if you were a healthy, ambitious young man with
a good eye for business.

It wasn't long after giving up seafaring that Robert Cain
started to find his feet and establish himself in a trade, first as
a barman and soon after as a cooper and small-scale brewer.
In 1851 he is recorded in the census as a 'journeyman cooper'
and the fact that he had a trade is probably one reason he
was able to make progress when so many did not. Coopering
would undoubtedly have been a useful skill in a maritime

city such as Liverpool, where demand for casks was huge. But as a native of Cork, and a citizen of Liverpool, two cities famous for their breweries, Cain had other ideas. By 1851 he was already making a name for himself as a brewer.

Cain's decision to enter the brewing trade could hardly have been timed better. In the 1840s the British brewing industry was just settling down into a period of growth that would continue almost without faltering into the 1870s. More importantly though, the 1840s in Liverpool turned out to be a boom period for small beer houses, often operating out of back yards and domestic dwellings. The cost of setting up a beer house was low and brewing on a small scale could be managed at the same time as holding down another job. No doubt Cain continued working as a cooper for exactly this reason.

Brewing in the 1840s offered opportunities that had only recently become available. In 1830 the government, led by the Duke of Wellington, had passed a bill abolishing excise duty on beer and deregulating its sale. The consequence of this was that around 45,000 new beer houses sprang up around the country, some brewing in-house, some selling on beer produced by others. From a political point of view this was a populist move at a time when revolution was a real possibility in Britain.

Encouraging the growth of beer houses went down well in the country. The idea was that by removing controls on beer houses, which came somewhere below pubs in the brewing industry pecking order, prices would fall and the quality of beer would rise. The quality and supply of beer did rise in the second half of the nineteenth century, but it was the larger 'common' brewers who drove the market.

Generally defined as producing over 10,000 barrels a year, the common brewers led the way in terms of hygiene, efficiency and quality. From about 1850 onwards the thousands of small brewhouses gradually gave in to pressure from brewers like Bass, Tetley, Walker's of Warrington and of course Robert Cain.

In fact Cain's success as a brewer actually went against the general trend of the market, which would gradually force the small-scale brewers out of business or turn them into sales outlets for bigger concerns. But while most small brewers did not survive beyond the nineteenth century, the 1830 Beer Act certainly had a permanent effect on the number of outlets for beer and created an opportunity for prudent men such as Robert Cain to set themselves up in business. T. R. Gourvish and R. G. Wilson describe a 'dramatic' growth in the number of licences issued nationally after the 1830 Act: 'Within six months 24,324 licences had been taken out, and within eight years the number had almost doubled to 45,717. In town and countryside alike they proliferated.' Liverpool is singled out as an example of the 'debauch' at its most extreme. There, 800 beer houses were opened immediately after the Act came into force.[4]

By 1840 the initial surge of new licences had come to an end, but in Liverpool the sheer number of new beer houses had left the market wide open. The Act itself was tightened up in 1834 and 1840, effectively putting the brakes on the bottom end of the brewing industry. This was partly because beer houses never really lost their reputation for crime and depravity, and partly because of fears that they were places

4 T. R. Gourvish and R. G. Wilson, with research by Fiona Wood, *The British Brewing Industry, 1830–1980* (Cambridge: Cambridge University Press, 1994), p. 16.

where revolution was being plotted. As Gourvish and Wilson show, drunkenness increased after the 1830 Act and later restrictions, including raising excise duty and demanding character references for licensees, were brought in to control it. Even so, such measures were probably as much to do with middle- and upper-class fears about the labouring classes as they were a genuine attempt to improve public order.

The growth in the number of private beer houses gradually slowed and then declined in the 1850s and 1860s, while the larger commercial brewers thrived. The beer houses never really managed to compete with the more restricted public houses, and Cain was lucky to enter the industry before the rise of the common brewers effectively blocked the progress of small operations. Yet his story is typical of most of the large regional brewers who dominated the local industry after the 1870s. Gourvish and Wilson describe the growth of breweries such as Cain's: 'They all grew on the same lines: a recent history, sometimes from public or beer house brewing origins; rapid growth after the 1860s, initially in the local free trade; application of the latest brewing techniques and breweries constantly expanded and rebuilt'.[5] But while Cain's brewing business followed the pattern of similar businesses of the time, many of the reasons for his success were specific to Liverpool and to his own personal situation.

By the 1840s Liverpool was already a lucrative market for both local and more distant brewers. The port made raw materials easily available and enjoyed good warehousing and good links by sea to other British towns. In the years before the railways, ships were the easiest way of transporting beer

5 Gourvish and Wilson, *The British Brewing Industry*, pp. 124–25.

around the country, and Liverpool became a distribution point for many brewers including Bass from the Midlands, Guinness from Dublin and Tetley from Leeds. While Cain's remained a Liverpool-centred company, competition meant that the established Liverpool market was dynamic and thriving, with plenty of room for new entrants. As far back as 1830 Michael Thomas Bass had opened an agency in Liverpool to sell his beer to local beer houses and pubs. By 1846, helped along by the spread of the railways, almost 7 per cent of Bass's sales – around £9,000 – were in Liverpool, while others such as Worthington, Allsopp, Tetley and Glasgow-based Youngers also had agents there, selling mostly bottled beer to beer houses and pubs.

Liverpool was famous for its large number of pubs and beer houses. The overcrowded living conditions made pubs a haven and a meeting place, while the poor quality of the drinking water made beer an essential part of the diet for rich and poor alike. One of the great concerns of Dr Duncan, Liverpool's Medical Officer in the 1840s, was to improve the water supply, and when the wells in Bootle and Toxteth Park proved unable to cope with the famine immigrants in the late 1840s, he campaigned for the use of reservoirs further afield in Lancashire to help improve the situation. Following the Liverpool Water Act of 1847, which allowed the city to take water from outside its boundary, a reservoir was proposed for Rivington Pike, an area of Lancashire moorland 30 kilometres to the northeast.

Despite the obvious problems with the water supply, the Rivington reservoir scheme divided opinion. Opponents of 'The Pike', including the newspaper *The Liverpool Mercury*, continued to campaign for an alternative to be found even in the face of mounting evidence that Liverpool was desperate for fresh water. Salt water from the Mersey was suggested as an alternative for public baths, for dust laying and for the sewers. Then on 12 January 1849 the *Mercury* reported that the Rivington project had been 'suspended at last'. The paper reminded readers of its campaign to find out 'whether or not we possess, or can immediately obtain, in our own neighbourhood, an ample supply of water for the inhabitants of this great town'.

Unfortunately the amount of water that could be found was not the only problem. Just two weeks later, on 30 January, the *Mercury* reported that the Board of Health had found two cases of cholera, one in the town and one in the hinterlands of West Derby. This was a major blow, but at that time nobody had linked infected water with cholera, so much of the debate about the disease centred on cure rather than prevention. The cholera outbreak in Liverpool later that summer was part of a pandemic that killed over 33,000 people in Britain and many more in cities across Europe.

In 1857, a decade after the scheme was proposed, the first water arrived in Liverpool from 'The Pike'. But still there were objections. The water, which contained peat from the moors, was brown, and there still wasn't enough of it. Liverpool continued to suffer water shortages and interruptions to supply. Drought and disease in 1865 meant that by 1866 the city's water engineers began looking for other places for reservoirs, in Wales, the Lake District and elsewhere in the Lancashire Pennines. Liverpool's water supply problems would not be resolved until the 1890s, when the controversial Vrnwy reservoir in North Wales was completed.

In an overcrowded city that relied on limited and often

filthy surface water and wells for its drinking water, beer was a natural substitute. Beer had the added benefit of being a source of energy for workers in manual jobs and was often provided for those in heavy industries such as iron foundries and shipbuilding. Water was a problem even among the wealthy inhabitants of the large houses springing up around Sefton Park, in Birkdale near Southport, and at Hoylake on Wirral. Several local brewers, including Aspinall's of Birkenhead, and the Phoenix Brewery of Leeds Street, advertised beer by the barrel on the front pages of newspapers such as the *Mercury*, aiming it specifically at private houses rather than pubs. In the 1840s beer was still regarded as having health benefits. Even the temperance movement, which was already waging a vigorous campaign against alcoholic drinks, did not object in the 1840s to the weak beer that was central to the diet of most Victorians.

Perhaps even before giving up his seafaring career in the late 1840s, Robert Cain had met Ann Newall, the daughter of James and Mary Newall formerly of Lowton, near Wigan in Lancashire, where Ann was born. Ann's father was a shoemaker. Robert and Ann were married on 4 April 1847 in St Philip's Church, Hardman Street, when Ann was just 17 years old; she is recorded as a minor on their marriage certificate. Like his father, Robert was illiterate and unable to sign his name, so he left his mark – a simple cross – on the marriage certificate instead.

The precarious economics of running a beer house or small pub demanded hard work and a certain amount of sacrifice. One story about how the Cains came to buy their first pub highlights how tight things were. Robert had returned from sea and announced that he wanted to set up in business. He had been putting money aside but decided to undertake one more voyage to raise enough money to buy a beer house. Ann revealed that she had been saving too and gave him £1, which was enough. Near the end of her life, not long before Robert Cain and Sons was incorporated in 1896, Ann claimed that the value of the company was £1,000,001. Ann's support for her husband was no doubt a key factor in the success of the business. Later in life Cain became well known in Liverpool as an early riser. He worked 13-hour days even in the 1890s, starting work at 5 o'clock in the morning and knocking on the doors of brewery workers to make sure they were at work on time. He claimed to be happiest when at home or inside the gates of the brewery. For him business, and in particular brewing, was an exciting and enjoyable challenge.

The combination of Cain's willingness to work hard, his natural talent for brewing, for selling, and for the physical demands of running a brewery would probably have made him a successful brewer anywhere. But in the dynamic atmosphere of Liverpool in the 1840s and 1850s he became an outstanding one. Within two decades the Cains would be settled in a large house busy with domestic staff in a fashionable part of town. Explaining his success in business, Cain said that in his experience the first few hundred pounds were the hardest: 'for as soon as the capital begins to work itself the money making begins in earnest'.[6] For Cain that moment came in 1850 when he was able to buy a small brewery on Limekiln Lane.

6 *Liverpool Review*, 1887.

2

Citizen Cain

In 1850 Robert Cain was a young man of 24 with a wife and growing family to support. He worked hard on his new brewing business and seems to have had a talent for making property deals as well as for promoting and selling his beer. In mid-nineteenth-century Liverpool, where poverty, lack of education and prejudice against upstart Irishmen all stood in his way, such skills gave him a head start in the city's tough environment. Cain had two things in mind as he began to have some success with his business. First, he wanted to build a business that would support him and his family. But he also wanted to escape the limitations of the Irish ghetto and transform himself into a Victorian gentleman.

The purchase of the brewery on Limekiln Lane in 1850 is generally regarded as the founding moment in the Cain's brewing tradition, but it also marks the point at which Cain began his long personal reinvention. Like brewing itself, a semi-mystical process that transforms ordinary materials – barley and hops – into something altogether more interesting, Cain transcended his own ordinary beginnings and became one of Liverpool's most influential men. This was an immigrant experience particular to its time and place. For many Irish immigrants the culture of their homeland held back their ambitions, and Robert Cain saw that one way to fulfil his dreams was to leave behind his fellow Irish and remake himself in the English mould. Victorian Liverpool proved surprisingly willing to go along with his plan.

Cain spent long hours in the brewhouse doing work that was physically as well as mentally demanding. He also showed remarkable adaptability, buying and selling pubs, working as a publican and hotelier, and seems to have continued in his trade as a cooper long after the brewing business was established. Cain took advantage of Liverpool's dynamic economy and vibrant street life, but the pattern of his success also matches that of the city. Over the course of the next fifty years, while Cain established a place for himself among the city's merchant ruling class, Liverpool threw off its 'black spot on the Mersey' reputation and became a centre for financial services, manufacturing, and home to the great shipping lines, including White Star and Cunard.

In the 1850s science, technology and engineering prowess came to define Britain in the eyes of the world. From the Great Exhibition of 1851, which showed off the country's abilities in science and the arts, to the publication of Charles Darwin's *On the Origin of Species* in 1859, the decade embodied the spirit of the Victorian age. Confidence in Britain's position as a world power was growing and Liverpool thrived on the new opportunities that came with it. Many of the most influential companies of the following century were founded in Liverpool in the 1850s including, in 1850, Royal Liver Assurance and in 1856 the first branch of David Lewis's department store chain. The decade also saw the construction of many of Liverpool's most important civic buildings, among them St George's Hall and the Free Library and Museum. By the end of the decade Liverpool was not only Britain's second city in terms of the insurance industry, finance and shipping, but it was also the second city of the British Empire, a dominant force in Europe, and able to stand alongside New York, Lisbon and Marseilles as one of the major maritime cities in the world.

Apart from British colonies and dominions, Liverpool was central to trade with the United States. As early as the mid-1840s, Liverpool merchant William Brown is estimated to have controlled around 15 per cent of Anglo-American trade. The economy and population of the United States were growing fast as the country blundered towards civil war and Liverpool took advantage of the huge cotton and grain markets that were opening up. In 1850, when California was admitted to the Union as the 31st state, Liverpool shipping lines were advertising passage to the West Coast gold fields. The same year, as Liverpool's population swelled with hundreds of thousands of migrants, Los Angeles officially became a city with a population of just 1,600 people. Though Liverpool was still growing at a frantic pace, the pressure caused by the Irish famine was beginning to ease back from its peak of 1847, especially as the city began to adapt to its larger population. In Europe the revolutions of 1848 had failed to trigger similar uprisings in Britain and on the whole the 1850s proved a period of relative stability and certainty. Even the Crimean War, which destabilised much of central Europe, proved profitable for Liverpool traders.

In the arts a century of Romanticism was drawing to a close, marked by the deaths of the poet William Words-worth in 1850 and the painter J. M. W. Turner in 1851.

Art and literature became more philosophical and more psychological as the century progressed. American author Nathaniel Hawthorne, who later served as American Consul in Liverpool, published his masterpiece *The Scarlet Letter* in 1850, while in Britain Charles Dickens was at the peak of his powers, completing the serialisation of *David Copperfield* that year. Dickens would visit Liverpool in 1858 to give acclaimed readings from his best-known works, including extracts from 'A Christmas Carol'.

Cain's own tastes were very much in line with up-to-date Victorian ideas. Through the architecture of his brewery and pubs he showed an interest in the most contemporary styles. Like many Victorian industrialists, Cain had a keen interest in the arts and in later years the Cain household seems to have been a place where music and painting were regular activities. In the 1870s the Cain family played host to William Daniels, a celebrated Liverpool portrait painter. As with his approach to business, technology and opportunity, Robert Cain was a Victorian to the core.

Most accounts of this period in the history of Robert Cain and his brewing business suggest that the Limekiln Lane brewery was the start of Cain's property-owning career. But he seems already to have owned several properties in the city and soon acquired more. Although Cain began brewing at Limekiln Lane in 1850 the family did not live on the brewery premises. At the time of the census in 1851 the Cains were living at 6 Ann's Terrace, in what was probably a beer house. Cain was registered to vote at 22 Limekiln Lane in 1854 and was still living there in 1855, though by then the brewing operation had moved to Wilton Street.

Limekiln Lane is in Vauxhall, not far from Scotland

Road. In the mid-nineteenth century it was at the centre of Irish Liverpool. The streets around Scotland Road had a reputation for wild behaviour, heavy drinking and, by the 1850s, a deep-seated sectarian tension between Catholics and Protestants. In their essay 'Cosmopolitan Liverpool' in *Liverpool 800*, John Belchem and Donald MacRaild point out that this became a feature of Liverpool politics in the second half of the nineteenth century. Liverpool was unusual in this respect: 'the sizeable presence of Ulster Protestants, a catalyst absent in most other English towns, served to activate latent British anti-Catholicism ... Orangeism was soon incorporated into the local Tory narrative of providential Protestant religious and constitutional freedom, attesting to British allegiance ...'[7] The Scotland Road ghetto had a pub on every corner, some of which were meeting places for extremist groups on both sides. And as the famine brought many more poor and starving migrants into Liverpool, the Irish developed a reputation for choosing to live off the Corporation. Newspaper cartoons showed starving Irish immigrants arriving in rags and leaving a few years later fat and healthy. Many people in Liverpool believed that the Irish chose to be dirty, lazy and immoral and there was a great deal of prejudice against them. Violence between Irish factions and between the Irish and the 'native' Liverpudlians was common and as a precaution around 2,000 troops were permanently stationed in the Everton area to help keep the peace.

Hostility towards the Irish grew and became entrenched in the 1850s. Many middle-class Irish immigrants realised

7   John Belchem and Donald M. MacRaild, 'Cosmopolitan Liverpool', in John Belchem (ed.), *Liverpool 800: Culture, Character and History* (Liverpool: Liverpool University Press, 2006), p. 327.

that keeping a distance from the slums of Scotland Road was an important part of being accepted into the city's elite. There were a few Irish merchants who helped support Liverpool Irish projects, including Richard Shiel, who tried to help Irish immigrants find their feet in the city, while Irish doctors, lawyers and educators often worked directly with the migrant communities. But as Belchem and MacRaild suggest, the Liverpool and Lancashire establishment preferred its members to be good English Anglicans, so figures such as William Brown dropped their Irish background and became Liverpool men. In Brown's case this expressed itself through funding the Liverpool Museum, which is decribed by Belchem and MacRaild as 'an immortalizing symbol of the culture of commerce in the "Florence of the North"'.[8]

Before long Robert Cain would also move away from Irish Liverpool and become a respected member of the city's Tory elite. But in 1850 he was very much a part of the community that centred on Scotland Road. After their marriage in 1847 Ann became pregnant almost immediately with the couple's first son, Robert James Cain, who was born on 10 January 1848. They also had a daughter, Hannah, who was born in 1850. Money must have been short for the young family and Cain took his responsibilities seriously. The *Liverpool Review* describes how he ran the brewery:

> Instead, therefore, of leaving the management and responsibility of his business to others he was in constant attendance at his brewery. The continuous fermentation going on in a brewery demands unceasing care and watchfulness, and consequently the work may be said to proceed night

8 Belchem and MacRaild, 'Cosmopolitan Liverpool', p. 332.

and day without interruption. Mr. Cain's working day began then, as it does even yet, before most people have entered their second sleep. In those days it extended over thirteen hours – from five in the morning till six at night. The necessities of the brewery, however, frequently demanded even closer attendance than this. A brewery is much the same as a steamboat, any breakdown must be promptly repaired at any sacrifice of time and comfort; and so it often happened that in addition to his regular thirteen hours a day Mr. Cain would be compelled to remain far into the night and even through the night.[9]

To keep costs down, Cain not only worked as his own head brewer but also handled the purchasing of ingredients and managed the sale and distribution of the beer. Within a few years of starting his brewery Cain owned several beer houses and pubs, which he supplied from his own brewery. He continued to expand his collection of houses throughout the 1850s, taking on the work of a salesman, a supply manager and a quality control inspector as well as that of head brewer.

By 1854, the year that Lord Aberdeen's coalition government took Britain into the Crimean War, the brewery in Limekiln Lane was no longer able to cope with the demand for Cain's beers. He purchased a larger brewery on Wilton Street, at a stroke doubling the number of 'hands' he employed and the amount of beer he produced. By then his capital was beginning to 'work itself' and the Limekiln Lane premises were leased and later sold to brewers David and Mathew Warriner. Cain's business kept expanding and in 1858 he was able to purchase an established brewery on Stanhope Street, where Cain's beers are still brewed one hundred and fifty years later.

9 *Liverpool Review*, 17 September 1887.

The Stanhope Street site offered space to expand, and it had its own good-quality water supply and existing equipment. But the move from the 'North End' ghetto to south of the city centre was also a move away from Cain's Irish beginnings and possibly even his family. Certainly the purchase of the Stanhope Street brewery was an indication of his ambition and of his determination to escape the poverty of his past. By then Robert and Ann Cain had four children. Besides Robert James and Hannah, Mary had been born in 1854 and a second son, Alfred Dean Cain, was born in 1856. Two more daughters, Sarah and Maria, would arrive in 1859 and 1861.

In the year of Maria's birth the Cains were living not far from the brewery at 3 Stanhope Street, which was then the Transatlantic Hotel and is now a pub called The Coburg. It appears that the Cains ran the hotel as part of the business, with Robert as the licensee and Ann's mother, by then a widow, living with them in the capacity of housekeeper. The family employed two live-in general servants and shared their property with Thomas Thomson, a barman. Although Cain's business was doing well by then, the Transatlantic Hotel was not a grand establishment. Being close to the docks and surrounded by warehousing and other industrial buildings it was probably a cheap residential hotel for single men – sailors and labourers – who needed a place to stay while working away from home.

In the 1860s many of the properties in the residential area around Stanhope Street were 'courts' where people lived in terrible conditions. Many of these were bought and demolished by Cain as he developed the brewery. While they already owned several properties around the city by 1861, including the brewery itself and The Grapes Inn, known since 1993 as The Brewery Tap, the Cains do not seem to have been in a position to own a house separate from the business. A frugal and clear-headed businessman like Cain may have been uncomfortable with such an extravagance having just taken on the Stanhope Street brewery, but he was already thinking about his position among Liverpool's merchant class and distancing himself from his Irish roots. In 1861, for the first time, the census lists Cain with Liverpool as his birthplace rather than Cork. The fact that his wife resolutely kept her correct birthplace on the official records suggests this was not done by mistake. Cork does not appear again on Cain's census returns: his transformation had begun.

The transformation of Liverpool was also well underway. St George's Hall was completed in 1854, providing a home for Liverpool's Crown Court as well as a magnificent concert hall and meeting rooms. In his notebook entry for 25 March 1855 Nathaniel Hawthorne wrote: 'St. George's Hall – the interior hall itself, I mean – is a spacious, lofty, and most rich and noble apartment, and very satisfactory. The pavement is made of mosaic tiles, and has a beautiful effect.'[10] The huge scale of St George's Hall, which ranks as one of the most important Victorian buildings in Britain, was in keeping with Liverpool's status and demonstrated to the world that the city was confident, wealthy and powerful. It was designed by Harvey Lonsdale Elmes, but completed by his advisor C. J. Cockerell after Elmes's death in 1847 at the age of just 33. Elmes had won the competition to build the hall

10 Nathaniel Hawthorne, *Passages from the English Notebooks of Nathaniel Hawthorne* (Boston: Houghton Mifflin, 1883), p. 42.

in 1839 with a strict budget of £30,000, but the eventual cost in 1854 was over ten times that amount.

The building, with its dramatic façade and wide paved 'plateau' extending onto Lime Street itself, quickly became a focal point for celebrations of all kinds. In December 1857 two guns captured in the battle for Sebastopol were awarded to the city by the government and placed outside St George's Hall. They were later moved to Wavertree Park and replaced with statues of Prince Albert and Queen Victoria as well as memorials to Liverpool's most influential and important citizens. Over the years St George's Hall has played host to the city's largest public celebrations, from the homecoming of troops from war and football teams fresh from victory, to New Year's Eve festivities.

Lime Street Station, with the first of its two curved iron roofs already in place, faced St George's Hall so that almost the first thing railway passengers saw of Liverpool was the hall's great frontage. The heavy neo-classical columns provided a sense of permanence and history to match the lightweight modern elegance of the station's great arcing roof. Developments near to St George's Hall in the 1850s further enhanced Liverpool's reputation as a cultural centre. On 15 April 1857 the foundation stone for William Brown's Free Library and Museum was laid in front of a large crowd. Invited guests, including Brown himself, other civic dignitaries and Hawthorne in his capacity as American Consul, processed from the Town Hall up James Street, Lord Street and Lime Street, which were lined with policemen. Hawthorne describes the scene in his notebook entry for 19 April, commenting that the weather was fine and sunny, which was 'a blessing which cannot be overestimated; for we should have been in a strange trim for the banquet, had we been compelled to wade through the ordinary mud of Liverpool'. Hawthorne goes on to describe the ceremony:

> ... when we came within the enclosure, the corner-stone, a large square of red freestone, was already suspended over its destined place. It has a brass plate let into it, with an inscription, which will perhaps not be seen again till the present English type has grown as antique as black-letter is now. Two or three photographs were now taken of the site, the corner-stone, Mr. Browne, the distinguished guests, and the crowd at large; then ensued a prayer from the Bishop of Chester, and speeches ...[11]

The subsequent banquet in St George's Hall was attended by 900 of the city's most influential people and concluded with speeches in praise of William Brown and his generous gift to the city. Hawthorne, who rarely enjoyed events of this kind, commented that the banquet 'hardly justified that name, being only a cold collation, though sufficiently splendid in its way. In truth, it would have been impossible to provide a hot dinner for nine hundred people in a place remote from kitchens.'

The excitement and clamour surrounding the beginning of work on the Library and Museum is an indication of the pride Liverpudlians felt for their city and the belief that Liverpool was ready to take its place among the world's greatest. The development of the area around St George's Hall eventually came to include the Free Library and Museum, the Walker Art Gallery, and St John's Gardens with its statues of Liverpool's 'great men'. This was the city's answer to 'Albertopolis', Prince Albert's collection of museums and galleries

---

11 Hawthorne, *Passages from the English Notebooks*, p. 154.

in South Kensington, London.

Yet Hawthorne's comment about mud is a reminder that in the 1850s Liverpool was still very much a city in transition. It was a great trading city, certainly, with a generous and growing share of successful businesses and opportunities. The end of the second Opium War in 1857 opened up China as a new trading destination, while in 1858 the newly formed Mersey Docks and Harbour Board took over control of the port of Liverpool, including the brand new Landing Stage off the Prince's Pier. The presence of the USS *Niagara* in the Mersey in the early part of the year, there to collect half of the Atlantic telegraph cable from the manufacturer in Birkenhead, hinted at greater possibilities to come. But although it was expanding at a rapid pace, the city's roads and other infrastructure had not yet developed to meet the demands placed upon them.

The amount of business activity going on in the city is reflected in the pages of the newspapers of the time. In the 1850s newspapers such as the *Mercury* carried several pages of advertisements on their front and inside front pages. These ranged from advertisements for shipping lines offering passage across the Atlantic, to theatre productions, notices of births, deaths and marriages, and classified ads. In January 1858 the *Mercury* carried a notice placed by a group of exasperated tailors encouraging the 'Men of Liverpool' to 'Begin the New Year well by paying your Tailor's bills'. Aspinall's of Birkenhead, a brewery that also acted as an agent for breweries elsewhere and specialised in supplying private houses, advertised 'Pale Ale, Prestonpans beer and mild pale ale to "private families". India Pale Ale No.3 (similar to Burton) 36 gallons for 50s.'

One of the most striking things about newspaper advertising in Liverpool in this period is the number of public houses, brew houses and 'wine stores' available for let or purchase. For example, in January 1858 the *Mercury* carried a 'Wanted' notice: 'Wanted for rent or purchase a brewery of from five to eight barrels with stable and yard attached'. Also advertised in the 20 January edition, at around the time that Cain was looking for new premises, was a brewery to let 'in the centre of Liverpool, 25 barrels in length, fitted up on the most approved principle to economize labour, with steam engine and plant complete and now in working order'. Brewing in Liverpool was clearly a popular business, but the number of sales and lettings also suggests that the failure rate was high. Cain's own experience before he bought the Stanhope Street brewery suggests that the market was fiercely competitive and that only the best breweries would survive and grow.

Cain bought the Stanhope Street brewery from George Hindley, the vicar of St George's church, Everton. George and Robert Hindley had inherited the brewery from their father. After his father's death Robert Hindley had tried and failed to make the brewery a success and was followed by Messrs Hyde and Rust, brewers, who rented the premises but lasted only a few months before they were forced out of business. Soon after acquiring the brewery Cain set about modernising and improving his investment:

> During the first two years of Mr. Cain's occupancy all the old brewing utensils and machinery were taken out and replaced with the most modern appliances. The place was thus carried on for some years when further increase of business necessitated an extension. This was effected by purchasing some of the adjoining property called 'Cotter's Terrace' and throwing

it into the brewery. An old building, containing offices and a warehouse, which originally stood in the yard was removed, and a new building, fronting Stanhope-street, was erected in its place. From the earliest time in Stanhope-street till the present moment Mr. Cain has been adding to and improving his brewing plant and machinery, and everything new which comes out and which is better than older machinery he buys without hesitation.[12]

Cain's willingness to keep up with developments and his commitment to relentless expansion and 'improvement' made the brewery a success where others floundered. The brewery itself had been bought by 'old Mr. Hindley' as a going concern seventy-two years earlier in 1786 so its long-term viability was not in doubt. But knowing its recent history of failure Cain must have been very confident in his own ability to make it work. He was certainly helped by Liverpool's own growing success story.

By the late 1850s Liverpool was benefiting from several significant events abroad. The city had been an important supply port during the Crimean War (1854–1856), when Western European armies fought to defend Turkey and to prevent Russia gaining a foothold in the Middle East. Although the resulting peace was an uneasy one, Britain, France and their allies succeeded in preventing the collapse of Turkey. More importantly the peace negotiations went a long way towards securing trade in the Mediterranean. The Crimean War was the first war in which steamships carried the bulk of the military supplies, and in the aftermath it was Liverpool steamship companies that were left with new opportunities for trade in the Mediterranean. Liverpool's global reach also expanded with the opening of new trade

12 *Liverpool Review*, 17 September 1887.

routes to China and to India, following the Government of India Act in 1858. The India Act followed the Indian War of Independence in 1857. It ended the British East India Company's reign, established direct British rule, and opened the continent to free trade.

The opening of the Suez Canal in 1869 was seen by some as a threat to Liverpool's dominance as a port, but developments in more efficient steam power by shipowners such as Alfred Holt of the Ocean Steamship Company (later the Blue Funnel Line) actually left the city at an advantage over its less-developed European rivals. The experience of building troop carriers in the mid-1850s also helped Laird's of Birkenhead to emerge as one of the world's greatest shipbuilders, while the Liverpool connection also benefited Belfast company Harland and Wolff as they became the shipbuilder of choice for Liverpool lines such as White Star.

The 1860s are generally regarded as the decade in which Liverpool entered its most dramatic period of growth and influence. The palm oil markets in West Africa, where Robert Cain spent his early adulthood making casks, grew dramatically with the arrival of steamships. As Graeme Milne explains, in the 1860s Liverpool became a trading hub in the 'first era of globalization'.[13] In tune with the city's fortunes, the 1860s also proved to be a decade of prosperity and growth for Cain and his brewery. For businessmen like him the 'liberal age' of Victorian Britain was one of opportunity and freedom. Even in brewing, always one of the most regulated and heavily taxed industries, the economic climate was improving. Under Prime Minister Lord Palmerston the duties on sugar, malt and hops were gradually reduced, hop

13 Graeme Milne, 'Maritime Liverpool', in Belchem (ed.), *Liverpool 800*, p. 261.

duty finally being abolished in 1863. And while brewers would have to wait until 1880 for duty on malt and sugar to disappear altogether – they were replaced by duty on the finished product – the effect was to make brewing a more attractive business prospect.

The decade began in Liverpool with the opening of the Free Library and Museum in 1860, but then in December 1861 the death of Prince Albert from typhus contracted at Windsor shocked the nation. Albert was a great favourite in Liverpool, where he had opened the Albert Dock in 1846 and where his idea of a Britain rich in art, science and design had been embraced by the city's planners and architects. But perhaps the biggest news of the year in Liverpool and around the world was the outbreak of the American Civil War.

The American Civil War began when eleven Southern states, where slave ownership was still common, broke away from the Union to form the Confederacy under the leadership of President Jefferson Davis. Initially the Union President Lincoln aimed simply to bring the breakaway states back into the Union, but in 1862 he announced that the abolition of slavery was also a reason for going to war with the South. This made it impossible for Britain and other European countries to give official support to the Confederate cause, and in fact Britain remained neutral throughout the conflict.

In Liverpool the war was a more difficult issue. As the one-time leading European port in the transatlantic slave trade, Liverpool had strong and long-standing links with the Southern states. These links had grown stronger after the abolition of the slave trade as the market for cotton grew in the mid-nineteenth century. By the time war broke out in April 1861, Liverpool was the destination for around 60 per cent of the cotton produced by the Confederate states. Cotton and sugar from the American South were a significant proportion of the imported goods coming through Liverpool, so the blockade of Southern ports had an immediate impact both on the city and further afield in Lancashire, where it caused what became known as the cotton famine. In response to this, Liverpool-born Prime Minister Gladstone offered work to unemployed mill workers on his Hawarden estate. Many Liverpool merchants and their families came out in favour of the Confederate cause, including the Laird shipbuilding family of Birkenhead.

While Liverpool suffered at first from the collapse of the cotton trade, in the long run the city exploited both the absence of American merchant vessels on the Atlantic trade routes and the Confederate states' need for warships. By the end of the war Liverpool shipping lines not only dominated the Atlantic, but had also opened up new cotton markets in the southern hemisphere as well as in Egypt and the Middle East. At a time when steamship passages to New York were offered with the reassurance that the ship would fly a 'neutral flag' to avoid being attacked, Liverpool allied itself firmly with the Confederates. The Confederacy's financial affairs were managed from offices in Rumford Place, not far from the Parish Church, while in 1864 the 'Lady Patronesses' of the Confederate Prisoners' Relief Fund placed an advertisement in *The Times* seeking support for a 'Bazaar' to be held in St George's Hall to raise money for Confederate prisoners. The Bazaar was held on 18 October and raised £20,000 in just five days, an enormous sum in the 1860s.

But the most dramatic episodes in Liverpool's connection with the Confederacy are to do with warships: the CSS

Alabama, designed and built at John Laird's yard in Birkenhead and launched in 1862 under the name *Enrica*; and the CSS *Shenandoah*, built on the Clyde. Both the *Alabama* and the *Shenandoah* were built as cargo vessels and converted to warships while at sea, though it is certain that the owners of the shipyards concerned knew what their real purpose would be. *Alabama* was commissioned by the Confederate 'spy', James Bulloch, who was based at Rumford Place, Liverpool. Despite protests from the United States Consulate, the ship was launched as the merchant vessel *Enrica* on 14 May 1862. It was widely known in Liverpool that the *Enrica* was to become a Confederate warship and there was no problem finding a willing crew among Liverpool's seamen. The *Enrica* was converted in the Azores and raised the Confederate flag on 24 August 1862, becoming the CSS *Alabama*.

Liverpool's reputation as a place where Confederates would receive sympathetic treatment is highlighted further by the case of the CSS *Shenandoah*. The *Shenandoah*'s commander, Captain Waddell, evaded capture for a whole year while being pursued by Union cruisers, sinking 38 ships during the twelve months he was at sea. Waddell continued to attack whalers even after the official end of the war. Knowing he would receive a hostile reception wherever he went, he brought the *Shenandoah* into the Mersey on 6 November 1865 and lowered the Confederate flag in surrender. *Shenandoah* was sold at auction by the American authorities in Liverpool.

Stories such as those of the *Alabama* and the *Shenandoah* caused consternation elsewhere in Britain. *The Times* accused Captain Waddell and his crew of piracy and reflected that 'In a certain sense it is doubtless true that the Shenandoah was built and manned in fraud of our neutrality, for those who gave the order for her construction and engaged her crew must have been well aware of her real destination'.[14] But for Liverpool, the American Civil War had been a great boost to trade. Apart from the initial 'cotton famine', Liverpool merchants, shipowners and traders did well from the war.

In Liverpool itself the 1860s saw improvements in housing, sanitation and transport. The recommendations made by Dr Duncan in the 1840s had led to serious efforts to make the city a healthier, more pleasant place to live, and many of these were beginning to pay off. Liverpool pioneered public bath houses in the 1830s when Catherine Wilkinson and her husband led a campaign to have them provided by the Corporation, and the first of many public washhouses in Britain opened on Upper Frederick Street in 1842. After the misery of the 1840s and the Sanitary Act of 1847, by 1860 the Liverpool Corporation had built around 160 miles of drains and sewers. Rules were laid down for minimum floor areas and window sizes in new houses. In *Duncan of Liverpool*, W. M. Frazer paraphrases James Newland the borough engineer:

> Large numbers of persons were removed from cellars ... the paving of streets, alleys and courts was much improved; scavenging was more efficiently performed; water hydrants were multiplied ... by-laws for the regulation of slaughter-houses were made and enforced; public conveniences were erected; habitable cellars were registered and put under control ... knackers' yards were placed under control; the nuisance from smoke was abated; and interment in pits was prevented ...[15]

14 *The Times*, 8 November 1865.

15 W. M. Frazer, *Duncan of Liverpool* (London: Hamish Hamilton, 1947; repr. Preston: Carnegie Publishing, 1997), p. 107.

Frazer concludes that this 'was truly the Golden Age of sanitation'. By the 1860s the mud that Hawthorne commented on with such distaste was disappearing from Liverpool's streets, living conditions were getting better, and the city's death rate was falling. Although diseases such as typhus and tuberculosis still killed hundreds of people in Liverpool every year, and a cholera outbreak in 1866 brought back unpleasant memories, the situation was improving.

A sign of Liverpool's willingness to improve was the number of developments that were firsts in Britain. For example, the borough needed to improve its transport infrastructure and fought for permission to set up a tram network. In 1868 it was granted an Act of Parliament to do so. In 1869 St Martin's Cottages were opened as the first corporation housing in Britain. Liverpool also pressed on with plans for its parks and gardens. In 1867 plans for Stanley Park were accepted and work also began on Sefton Park, one of the largest urban parks in England. The construction of Sefton Park provided employment for 1,000 men and took five years. Everywhere new warehousing was being built, new docks, churches and schools were opening, and Liverpool was growing into a modern Victorian city.

For Robert Cain and his family, the early 1860s were the period in which they began to enjoy their success. Benefiting from the abolition of duty on hops, Cain made constant improvements to the brewery and expanded the number of tied houses. The pace of change at the brewery was dramatic. From the tiny brewery on Limekiln Lane in 1850, by the early 1860s Cain was no longer able to manage every aspect of the business himself. By then the brewery was producing around 200 barrels of beer every week and was growing fast.

On 14 July 1862 he engaged a young brewer, William Black-burn, who stayed with the company for the next five years and helped develop some of Cain's most distinctive beers, including the celebrated XXXX ale.

The death of Robert and Ann's two-year-old daughter Maria in 1863 was followed the same year by the birth of another daughter, Lena, and on 7 May 1864 a son, William Ernest Cain. By 1866, when Charles Alexander Cain was born, the family had moved into a villa called 'Mersey View' in Grassendale Park, an exclusive Victorian enclave several miles outside the city. William and Charles would go on to become the joint directors of the company Robert Cain and Sons Ltd after their father's death, and later took charge of Walker's of Warrington. Both received knighthoods and in 1933 Charles entered the House of Lords with an hereditary peerage and became known as Lord Brocket.

The move to Grassendale Park was a significant one for the Cain family, not only because of the way it changed how they lived, but also for what it represented. Grassendale Park in the 1860s offered wealthy families a retreat from the city's noise and grime, and when the Cains lived there the enclave was separated from the city by open fields. Sefton Park and the grand houses around it had not yet been built, while to the east Garston was a farming community. The houses in Grassendale Park are large and most stood in their own grounds. One of the attractions of Grassendale Park is the Esplanade, a promenade that runs along the bank of the Mersey, backed by large Victorian villas facing across the river. It is easy to imagine Ann Cain and her growing children taking walks along the Esplanade, or looking at the view from their large picture windows. In a little over ten years they had come a very long way from Limekiln Lane.

Even in the 1860s Grassendale was a convenient com-
muting distance from the city. Cressington station, which
opened in 1864, handled trains that would have taken
commuters into Liverpool in just a few minutes, passing
through Aigburth and St Michaels. But Robert Cain chose
to travel to the brewery every day on his horse, setting off
long before the first train was running to begin work at 5
a.m. Cain's regular work habits gained him a reputation in
Grassendale and Aigburth where the sound of his horse's
hooves became as important to some people as the chiming
of the church clock. The *Liverpool Review* takes up the
story:

> Mr. Charles Challoner, who lived in ... [Aigburth] Hall used
> to hear the sound of a horse trotting past in the early grey
> hours of the morning, and at length enquired about the
> person from the sexton of Grassendale Church. 'He goes
> past like the clock', said Mr. Challoner. 'I have looked at the
> time over and over again when his horse passed and he was
> almost invariably to the same minute. I never need to look at
> my watch in the morning now, I know the exact time by Mr.
> Cain's horse's hoofs.'[16]

For all of the attractions Grassendale had to offer, the journey
into Liverpool must have been difficult, especially in winters
such as 1866, when the snowfall was heavy enough to bring
down telegraph wires. Despite the success of the business
Cain was still working 12- or 13-hour days, and continued to
do so well into his seventies.

16 *Liverpool Review*, 1887, p. 10.

3

Superior Ales and Stouts

In the space of two decades Robert Cain had moved his family away from Irish Scotland Road, first to Toxteth, then to Grassendale Park. In doing so he had embraced the tastes and values of Victorian England and begun his transformation into a Victorian gentleman. As the area around Sefton Park was developed after 1868 the Cains were tempted to move back into the city, and by 1872 they were living in a mansion called 'Barn Hey' on Aigburth Road and had taken their place among Liverpool's elite merchant families.

While his work ethic and tough-mindedness must have made him a formidable figure, Cain was also popular and much admired by his employees. So when he made the move back into the city it was as a man in control of his destiny and confident of his own opinions and position in the world. His brewery continued to expand and Cain's public houses were a familiar sight, especially in the area to the south of the city centre. He was also gaining influence in local politics and the move to Aigburth Road positioned him in the heart of Tory Toxteth.

A century later, in the 1980s, Liverpool was known as the most troubled and politically the most left-wing city in

Britain. It was a hotbed of militant trade unionism and by 1984 had fallen under the control of the Trotskyist element of the Labour Party, known as 'Militant Tendency'. But in the nineteenth century the city consistently returned Tory MPs and was governed by Tory councillors. This was despite the fact that Tory voters tended to move out to the suburbs which returned fewer councillors per head than the older, more established wards in the city centre.

Several important changes in Liverpool's social and political makeup took place in the 1860s and 1870s. First, the Reform Act of 1867 gave male householders the vote, making working-class men a significant force in British politics. Secondly, the Education Act of 1870 made free basic education available to all, increasing literacy and expanding the size of the skilled working class. Thirdly, the late nineteenth century saw the rise of an increasingly powerful temperance movement which was especially militant in Liverpool. Backed by several Christian groups, the temperance campaigners encouraged people to 'sign the pledge' and never drink again. Failing that, they wanted to put strict curbs on drinking and licensing hours and in the 1890s almost succeeded in bringing in prohibition.

Much to the disgust of brewers such as H. K. Aspinall of Birkenhead, temperance campaigners had a great deal of influence on the magistrates' bench and were an important factor in the licensing of new pubs. In his book *Anti-Booze Crusaders in Victorian Liverpool*, Tim Malcolm explains how Aspinall, a magistrate himself, was barred from presiding over licensing sessions and complained that if brewers were forbidden then those supporting temperance should also step aside.[17] Ironically, the temperance movement may actually have benefited the business and political interests of brewers such as Robert Cain. It gave local Tory brewers an opportunity to position themselves as the friend of the working man by defending the pub from those who wanted to destroy it. Cain's lasting legacy in Liverpool, besides the magnificent brewery and the beer that bears his name, are the ornately decorated pubs he built partly in an effort to clean up the image of the brewing industry. Drinkers in Liverpool's most celebrated pubs have the temperance movement to thank for their comfortable surroundings.

The period in which Robert Cain established himself as a brewer was the heyday of Victorian industry. While the country was being run by a series of weak minority governments, its figurehead, Queen Victoria, came to embody British power at home and abroad. The rituals and majesty of the monarchy contrasted with that other Victorian character type, the upstart industrialist entrepreneur, but as H. C. G. Matthew argues, it was a counterbalance not a point of conflict: 'The monarchy represented the timeless quality of what was taken to be a pre-industrial order. In an increasingly urbanized society, it balanced the Industrial revolution.'[18] As a brewer, a popular employer with a reputation for looking after his workers, and a member of the local Tory elite, Cain had considerable influence on the way Liverpool was run. For the first time in Britain the whole structure of society was being altered by industrial and urban interests rather than the aristocratic, rural ones of the past.

17 Tim Malcolm, *Anti-Booze Crusaders in Victorian Liverpool* (Birkenhead: Countyvise, 2005), p. 41.

18 H. C. G. Matthew, 'The Liberal Age, 1851–1914', in *The Oxford History of Britain* (Oxford: Oxford University Press, 2001), p. 549.

It was during the 1850s and 1860s that British businesses, especially in manufacturing, became the envy of the world. Self-made entrepreneurs such as Cain were held up as proof that the Victorian values of hard work, decency and moral toughness would be rewarded. Of course, the truth was that the economic strength of Victorian Britain, and the wealth of its industrialists, depended on the large supply of low-paid workers around the world, not least the thousands of Irish immigrants who worked on Britain's railways and canals. But the rise of British industry also brought with it a need for a whole new category of worker who was technically skilled and well educated. As a result, the Victorian era saw improvements in schools, public health and, through the construction of corporation housing, better places to live.

The brewing industry faced many challenges after the 1850s, from the political threat posed by the temperance movement to the rush to acquire tied houses. The late nineteenth century saw the gradual decline of the small pub-based brewers and the rise of powerful commercial brewers who not only controlled the brewing part of the business but also acted as landlord and lender to their tenant publicans.

Right from the start, property had been a major part of Cain's business. Even before the 1860s, when brewers began a frenzy of pub buying, he had started to build up his property holdings. Under the tied house system publicans, or 'Licensed Victuallers', paid rent to the brewer and borrowed from him to pay for the fixtures and fittings the previous tenant had left behind. The tied house system, which had been around for decades but really took hold in the 1860s and 1870s, also allowed brewers to dictate what was sold in pubs besides beer. Many, including Cain, sold spirits through their pubs and demanded that publicans took the drinks from them rather than from another supplier.

Such restrictive conditions did nothing to improve relations between brewers and their tenants, but it meant that brewers received a steady rental income regardless of the demand for beer. The purchase of tied houses was also a way of holding back competitors, since it reduced the number of available 'free trade' outlets. This became especially important after the railways made it possible for some brewers to sell beer on a national scale. David W. Gutzke, in his book *Protecting the Pub*, explains:

> The railway's impact, however, was uneven. Only certain breweries, especially brewers of pale ale, which travelled better and paid high profits, exploited burgeoning beer consumption in the 1860s–70s. Their movement into new distant areas antagonized local firms, which sought tied outlets as an alternative to larger outsiders gaining access to markets ...[19]

Cain's brewery, which remained Liverpool-centred throughout the nineteenth century, fended off rivals such as Warrington's Peter Walker and Sons, and the more distant Burton and London brewers with exactly this tactic. Between 1850 and 1900 Cain bought or built over 200 tied houses, most of them after 1870. Just as Liverpool's insurance and shipping industries found ways to make themselves competitive against larger companies from outside the city, so Cain built his brewery as a notably Liverpool concern.

Liverpool was exceptional in the mid-nineteenth century for the number of beer houses, pubs, wine vaults and gin

19 David W. Gutzke, *Protecting the Pub: Brewers and Publicans Against Temperance* (Woodbridge: Royal Historical Society, Boydell Press, 1989), pp. 20–21.

shops that lined its streets. In his aptly titled book *A Pub on Every Corner*, Freddy O'Connor explains that pubs and 'drinking dens' were everywhere in nineteenth-century Liverpool. Including private clubs, which were exempt from restrictions on opening hours, O'Connor gives a figure of almost 3,000 licensed premises in the city centre in the early 1860s:

> In 1865, the number of licensed premises, excluding clubs, was still 2,841. Many of these premises were not pubs as we know them today, often they were entered through shops, such as grocers or tobacconist, into dismal drinking dens and in many cases ... would not have been licensed.[20]

Clearly, neither the décor nor the beer in these establishments was of high quality. They catered for desperate people who lived in overcrowded conditions and were prepared to spend what little money they had on getting drunk. As O'Connor points out, although steps were taken to close down 'inferior' brewers, and to control the number of outlets for alcoholic drinks, it was not until the 1930s that the number of beer houses in Liverpool fell dramatically.

But while Liverpool's vast population of desperate poor drowned their considerable sorrows in filthy and unpleasant conditions, the more respectable pubs and hotels were beginning to look towards quality. Brewers such as Robert Cain, John Houlding and Daniel Higson, as well as the agents for breweries from outside the city, realised that they had to distance themselves from the seedier end of the market. Pressure from the temperance movement and the magistrates, and the rising cost of property, meant that after about

---

20 Freddy O'Connor, *A Pub on Every Corner, Volume One: The City Centre* (Liverpool: Bluecoat Press, 1995), p. 6.

1885 existing pubs and hotels were developed and improved rather than new ones built. By the late 1890s many pubs competed as much on the luxuriousness of their interiors as the quality of their beer, but it is worth considering here what kind of product Cain might have been making and selling in the second half of the nineteenth century.

The general process of converting malt into beer through the stages of mashing, boiling and fermentation is the same everywhere. But brewers are notoriously secretive about their techniques for combining water, malt and hops, the three main ingredients in beer. This makes it difficult to work out exactly what beer from the period was like. In the case of Cain's, however, evidence from the 1860s offers an insight into the style and quality of the beer being produced, as well as telling us quite a lot about the size of the brewery. This evidence takes the form of a ledger or brewer's diary kept by William Blackburn, who joined Robert Cain's brewery on 14 July 1862. For the next five years he brewed some of Cain's best-known beers and the 'Superior Ales and Stouts' that were advertised around Liverpool on billboards and pub signs. Blackburn's meticulous record includes details of the type, age and quantities of hops and malt used, as well as the outcome of each brew. The final brew Blackburn made for Cain took place on 7 September 1867, before he took up a position in the Windsor Brewery on Upper Parliament Street, which belonged to his family. He records sadly 'These brews were left in the squares when I left Cains and I do not know the result of them'.

In the mid-nineteenth century scientific approaches to brewing were in their infancy, though chemical analysis of water supplies was becoming common among the larger producers. The rate at which Cain's brewery expanded suggests that even then he was able to make reliable, uniform beer of good quality. William Blackburn records the rate of expansion in his ledger. When he first began working for Cain the brewery was producing around 53 or 54 barrels of beer every two or three days, up to around 150 barrels each week. Five years later production had risen to 64 barrels every other day. In some weeks in 1867, even during the difficult summer months, the brewery produced almost 300 barrels of finished ale each week, around 15,000 barrels a year. This was not a large brewery by national standards. London brewer Whitbread produced 190,000 barrels in 1830 and 250,000 in 1880. But the rate of growth – a doubling of output in just five years – is remarkable nevertheless. Later in life Cain became known for having a keen interest in the most up-to-date techniques and claimed that if he could see an advantage in a new piece of equipment he would buy it without hesitation. It is likely that, despite having limited formal education, Cain was already interested in brewing to modern scientific standards when he bought the Stanhope Street site.

The development of properly controlled brewing processes in the mid-nineteenth century also had an effect on the kinds of beer being brewed. The heavy brews of Georgian England gave way over time to the light pale ales popular in the late nineteenth century. By 1900 the quantity of hops used in brewing, and the amount of alcohol in beer, were much reduced. This was partly because tastes changed and drinkers demanded brighter, more refreshing beers, but it was also to do with the brewers' own abilities to control their processes, improve turnover and reduce costs. Gourvish and Wilson explain:

Every Georgian brewer – the London porter brewers very successfully – had retailed a thick, winter-brewed beer suited to local tastes. The art of brewing by the 1870s was to produce regularly throughout the year a wider range of quick-maturing beers, including light, bright ales – technically a much more difficult feat.[21]

Cain's fascination with the latest methods would have made his brewery both more efficient and more in tune with popular tastes than many of his competitors. And because of the growth of the railways in the 1840s, Cain's competitors were some of the most powerful brewers in the country.

The kinds of beer on offer in mid-nineteenth-century Britain ranged from London porters and the stouts and porters made by Guinness in Dublin, through to the lighter milds, bitters and pale ales from the Burton brewers. William Blackburn's ledger shows that Robert Cain was brewing a mix of porter, which he often flavoured with cayenne pepper, stout, bitter and mild, all divided into categories XX, XXX and XXXX, as well as '6d' (sixpenny) and '2d' (twopenny) ales. Later in the ledger, after he had left Cain's, Blackburn noted down an analysis of 'Liverpool water' for the Windsor Brewery which reveals that the relatively low quantity of calcium in Liverpool's water was similar to that found in Dublin's water supply. At 124 parts per million (Dublin's is around 119) this would have made Liverpool especially suitable for brewing heavier, sweeter, darker ales and stouts.

Calcium is an essential part of the fermentation process and higher levels of the mineral produce brighter, more

---

21 Gourvish and Wilson, *The British Brewing Industry*, p. 48.

bitter beers, such as those produced in Burton. Burton water contains almost twice the amount of calcium as that in the water in Blackburn's sample. Liverpool's water seems to have been quite high in sodium – enough to make for a sweeter, more rounded brew – and chloride. These two together of course form common salt, which is necessary in the production of sweeter, darker beers. In fact the sample Blackburn quotes suggests a level of saltiness that would have been quite noticeable in the drinking water at the time.

Liverpool's water seems to have been unusual, resulting in beers that were distinctive and particular to the city. At a time when Burton-style pale ales were beginning to dominate the country's pubs, the Scouse palate was clearly more accustomed to stouts than lighter beers. 'Liverpool exceptionalism', a term used by historians to describe the city's economic, social and political differences in comparison with the rest of the country, seems to have reached even as far as taste in beer.

The rise of pale ale is a good indication of how the brewing industry was changing in the mid-nineteenth century. India Pale Ale (IPA) was originally brewed to survive the harsh six-month sea voyage to the Indian colonies. It was heavily hopped and high in alcohol to make it less likely to go off on the journey. Before the railways existed, in the 1820s and 1830s, Burton brewers such as Bass and Worthington were already selling pale ales, particularly in port cities such as London and Liverpool. But the difficulties of transporting beer by canal or horse and cart made Burton ales a premium product enjoyed mostly by the middle classes. The railways changed all that. From being restricted by their lack of easy access to seaports, the landlocked Burton brewers soon found themselves at the centre of a railway network that gave fast, cheap and easy access to the entire country. Combined with better brewing techniques, which improved the stability of lighter beers, the national rail network soon turned Burton into Britain's dominant brewing centre.

By the late 1840s the popularity of Burton pale ales was growing fast and it continued to grow through the rest of the century. Robert Cain was not the only brewer whose business was doing well. According to K. H. Hawkins and C. L. Pass in their book *The Brewing Industry*, Bass's output grew so quickly between 1850 and 1865 that two additional breweries had to be built in the town.[22] And by 1867 Bass's new London store underneath St Pancras Station could house 120,000 barrels at any one time. This was almost 10 per cent of the entire annual output of all the Burton-based brewers put together, and eight times the output of Cain's brewery in that year.

The small town of Burton became famous for the quality of its water and at its peak in the 1880s boasted 30 large breweries. But it wasn't just ales brewed in Burton itself that were popular. Soon brewers all over the country were experimenting with the 'Burton Union' method of fermentation, first developed in Burton in the 1840s. As Gourvish and Wilson explain, this involved 'cleansing' the beer after about 36 hours of fermentation into 'union casks which allowed the carbon dioxide to expel the yeast through swan-necked pipes into yeast troughs. [...] Thought to be unparalleled for producing bright, pale ales, it was expensive in terms of casks, buildings, and cooling equipment.'[23] Because of these

22 K. H. Hawkins and C. L. Pass, *The Brewing Industry: A Study in Industrial Organisation and Public Policy* (London: Heinemann, 1979), p. 21.

23 Gourvish and Wilson, *The British Brewing Industry*, p. 57.

expenses by the 1990s only Marston's in Burton itself still brewed using the Burton Union method.

Although previous owners had failed to make the Stanhope Street brewery work for them, in fact it had several advantages as a site for large-scale brewing. For one thing it was located in a semi-residential area between the city and the rapidly growing suburbs of Toxteth. This made distribution of beer to Cain's growing chain of tied houses easier than it might have been. Just as importantly, Stanhope Street is close to the docks, ideally located for the supply of raw materials coming ashore.

It is most likely that, in the early days, Cain bought his malt from suppliers in East Anglia, where most of the British barley used in malting was grown. The quality of the malt used in brewing has a direct impact on the quality of the brew, and as a brewer with a good reputation Cain would have taken care to buy only the best malt he could find. Large brewers such as Courage, Whitbread and Bass solved the problem of finding quality malt by owning their own malt houses. A few brewers, including Whitbread, controlled the whole supply chain, from hundreds of acres of 'hop gardens' in Kent to private maltings in East Anglia. But for a small brewer, as Cain was in the 1850s and 1860s, it would have been more difficult. Blackburn's ledger records quantities of malt alongside names such as Hands, Harvey, Whitworth and Foster, suggesting that Cain was constantly reviewing and changing his suppliers and the types of malt he used to maintain quality and price.

Later, when British malt became much more expensive, foreign malt and barley were imported through Liverpool, and like many other breweries Cain's used California-grown ingredients. But even though new markets increased competition among suppliers, the difficulty of finding good-quality ingredients did not go away. Decades later, on 11 November 1913, the board of Robert Cain and Sons Ltd pondered the problem of finding a good supplier of malt when it was discovered that a regular supplier, Messrs Soames and Co., had been selling malt of inferior quality. The board asked Dr E. R. Moritz to examine the malt. Moritz was one of the most eminent figures in the science of brewing and an expert in the preparation of malt. He was the founder in 1886 of The Laboratory Club, an organisation set up to promote and carry out scientific research into brewing processes; it became known as the Institute of Brewing in 1890. Moritz's letter explains that the malt in question had been through many attempts to make it tender and he concludes, damningly: 'I do not like the malt'. It is recorded in the minutes of the meeting that 'Mr. Soames read the letter with which he did not disagree'. Soames did not supply the company again.

Malt and its substitutes was always one of the brewers' most difficult purchases. But there was one commodity the Stanhope Street brewery had in abundance which placed it ahead of most other breweries in Victorian Liverpool. In 1858 the brown but clean water from Rivington Pike had been available in Liverpool for less than a year. 'The Pike' supplied a very small number of streets and for most residents finding clean water was still a serious problem. For brewers of any size a plentiful and reliable supply of clean water was crucial. Gourvish and Wilson estimate that by 1900 it took 15 or 16 barrels of water to produce a single barrel of beer. Most of this water was used in cooling and washing and could be

taken from rivers and canals.[24] For actual brewing the supply
had to be clean and pollution-free, and for most brewers this
meant drilling wells, sometimes as deep as 250 metres. One
of the first improvements Robert Cain made to his brewery
was the development of the water supply. Cain used water
from his own well for brewing, and by the 1860s the brewery
drew water from an underground lake for cooling, steam
power and everything else.

The addition of the lake underneath the Stanhope Street
brewery gave Cain a distinct advantage over his rivals. Unlike
a well, which can run dry, or may need to be extended as
demand for water increases, the size of the Cain's lake meant
that it could provide a reliable and practically unlimited
supply of fresh water. This freed Cain from the expense
of buying water from the water companies and made the
brewery self-sufficient in its most important commodity. In
an industry where the price of raw materials could change
dramatically from one year to the next, having a steady and
guaranteed supply of water made Cain's success all the more
likely.

The lake itself has been the subject of a great deal of
speculation over the years. The Victorian fashion for Gothic
stories must have made the idea of a lake hidden beneath
the brewery an excellent source of tall tales. One such story
has it that after heavy rains, coffins were washed down
from St James's Cemetery, where the Anglican Cathedral
now stands, and were found bobbing around in the Cain's
lake. Another involves brewery workers rowing a boat by
lamplight across the still water. But despite Cain's enthusiasm for elaborate architecture and grand gestures, this was

24 Gourvish and Wilson, *The British Brewing Industry*, p. 49.

no Xanadu on the Mersey. The lake always had a practical and industrial purpose.

In an article in the local Campaign For Real Ale (CAMRA) magazine *Mersey Ale*, Paul Wilson, a manager at the brewery in the 1990s, describes uncovering the entrance to the Cain's lake:

> I descended on the ladder with the sump pump pipework adjacent to me, which was tight enough to mean that I was squeezing against this pipework for the descent of about 20 metres. The access then broke into a large cavern to which below me there was a wooden ladder leading to a wooden platform floating on an underground lake. I put my foot on the first rung of the ladder and it collapsed beneath me. I put my foot on the second rung and again it collapsed. There was no physical way down to the lake. However, it was obvious from shining the flashlight around the cavern that it was man made and had been hewn out of the sand-stone.[25]

An advanced cooling plant would have made year-round brewing possible, and Cain's interest in technological improvements would have made this an attractive idea. An editorial article in *Mersey Ale* a few months later reveals that the cavern was being developed in the 1860s. This must have formed part of Cain's redevelopment of the brewery site in the years after his purchase and explains Blackburn's output of 300 barrels per week in the summer of 1867:

> the wooden ladders had decayed leaving a 70 foot drop to the surface of the water. This was bridged with caving ladders and the use of abseiling techniques drawn from Pete's experience as Director of the Leader Outdoor Pursuits Centre. The large lake cavern was man made hewn from the surrounding

25 Paul Wilson, 'Mystery Lake Below Cain's Brewery Update', *Mersey Ale*, Winter 2004, p. 14.

sandstone. Indeed carved letters dated 1864 were found on the rock.[26]

The editorial goes on to describe two blocked-off tunnels, one containing pumping equipment and another going off up Stanhope Street towards the Cathedral. It ends: 'Unfortunately there was no sign of a boat'.

Besides malt and water the third main ingredient of beer is hops. Hops are added to the sweet malt solution before fermentation to improve the flavour and aromas of the finished beer, and also prevent the growth of harmful bacteria while allowing the yeast to survive. Hops add bitterness to balance the sweetness of the malt or sugars and are also believed to have a narcotic effect. E. A. Pratt, arguing against the temperance movement in *The Licensed Trade*, points out that the 'hop rate' of English beer had declined markedly over the previous generation, by which he means from about 1880. He explains the differences between different kinds of drunkenness:

> ... so the man who gets drunk on beer displays symptoms very different from those of the man who gets drunk on spirits. The latter may become readily violent and either be destructive – smashing windows, for example – or else quarrel with, or even attack, those around him. But the man whose drunkenness is due to beer becomes stupid rather than violent, and reels about, having, in effect, been 'narcotized' by the influence on his system of the hops in the beverage he has taken in excess. These conditions more especially prevailed a generation ago ...[27]

Part of the reason for the falling level of 'hopping' in beer was the rising price of hops and the volatility of the market.

26 *Mersey Ale* editorial, Spring 2005, p. 32.
27 Edwin A. Pratt, *The Licensed Trade: An Independent Survey* (London: John Murray, 1907), p. 229.

Many brewers stockpiled hops when the price was low and used them later when the price rose. But it was also caused by changes in taste as the heavier beers of the mid-nineteenth century gave way to the lighter, brighter, less alcoholic beers of the early twentieth century.

In the 1860s Robert Cain's Mersey Brewery was still producing heavily hopped beer, in line with local tastes. Gourvish and Wilson note that Bass's export beers 'contained as much as 5lb of hops per barrel in mid-century', but this had fallen to 1.9 pounds per barrel by 1900.[28] Bass is held up as an example of heavily hopped beer but Robert Cain's were very similar. On 8 June 1865 brewer Blackburn records a 'XXXX' ale brewed using 200 bushels of Whitworth malt, 140 pounds of yearling Kent hops and 120 pounds of yearling Hereford hops. This produced 57 barrels of ale at a rate of 4.5 pounds of hops per barrel and Blackburn describes it as 'A good fermentation, will turn out well'. Just a few months earlier, on 7 April, Blackburn recorded brewing a bitter ale and in comparison with the sweet XXXX ale it must have been very bitter indeed. This brew contained half as much malt – just 96 bushels of Whitworth – and 360 pounds of hops, divided equally between Jessops from Kent and Meredith from Hereford. This turned out 65 barrels at a rate of 5.53 pounds per barrel. This, Blackburn notes, 'Turned out beautiful beer'.

The use of year-old or 'yearling' hops was common among brewers. Older hops are milder in flavour than those that have been freshly harvested, which can have an unpleasant bitterness. They were also cheaper, but in the days before hops were easily available from overseas, brewers were dependent

28 Gourvish and Wilson, *The British Brewing Industry*, p. 194.

on the harvest from the previous year. However, Blackburn's ledger reveals that sometimes Cain was prepared to use hops that were very old indeed. Old hops seem to have been used most often in the lighter XX and XXX ales, but in December 1866 Blackburn brewed a heavy ale using Kent hops harvested ten years before. These were mixed with recent hops from Bavaria and Hereford and were presumably purchased at a knock-down price. Blackburn's comments on the success of his brews are usually positive, indicating a generally high level of quality and consistency even in mid-summer when the weather was against him. This time, however, he was well aware of the shortcomings of his materials. Although this was a good fermentation, he notes, it had 'too many old hops for bitter ale'.

The fastidiousness of Blackburn's record-keeping, which includes notes of when new equipment arrived at the brewery, suggests a high degree of organisation and a desire to control the processes and monitor the ingredients being used. This was scientific brewing by the standards of the time and, like any modern brewery, the Mersey Brewery was able to produce ale year-round. But despite having up-to-date equipment, including 'attemperaters' to keep the fermenting beer either cool or warm as the need arose, the weather still played its part. The winter of 1866–1867 was an especially harsh one, and while Robert Cain was fighting through the snow on horseback from Grassendale to Toxteth, William Blackburn was struggling in the brewhouse. Between 4 December and 29 December 1866, Blackburn records 15 separate brews. He worked Christmas Eve and Boxing Day and produced 311 barrels of beer in the week after Christmas. At the end of it all he says: 'The weather has been very severe of late. The warm attemperater has been used all the time the fermentation has been going, but the ale has turned out very fair.'

In many ways Robert Cain and his brewery were role models for Victorian industry. The brewery was a modern, technologically advanced operation, run by a man who saw the benefit in adopting every improvement the age had to offer. Yet, as Gourvish and Wilson point out in their chapter on 'Costs, prices, and profits', Victorian brewers were unique among entrepreneurs in that they were involved in both industrial manufacture and agriculture.[29] For many Victorians it was manufacturing and industry that embodied the spirit of the age. The great Victorian cities, among which Liverpool was one of the finest, were themselves evidence that through ingenuity, technical skill and industrial engineering, problems of housing, sanitation and transport could be addressed, if not entirely solved. But brewers 'faced both ways' in that their business depended on being up to date with the most advanced manufacturing processes, as well as having a less glamorous stake in the success of the harvest.

Brewers were also exceptional as manufacturers in that they were involved in retailing. Unlike shipbuilders, foundries or even mining companies, brewers were involved with their product from the creation of raw materials right through to the moment a drinker put a glass to his or her lips. This gave them a powerful sense of responsibility for areas of life where they personally would never dream of becoming involved. As Tim Malcolm points out, few wealthy brewers ever visited their own pubs. Yet they were bound to protect

29 Gourvish and Wilson, *The British Brewing Industry*, pp. 179–225.

them and did so in terms that suggested they were providing a public service, perhaps even a basic human right. Malcolm gives the example of H. K. Aspinall, the Birkenhead brewer, who was also chairman of the Mersey Ferry Committee. Aspinall warned that, having closed down the working-class pubs, anti-drink reformers might then make it compulsory for the keys to private wine cellars to be handed to the chief constable at weekends.[30]

Like other brewers, Cain fought hard against the restrictions on licensing and continued to buy licensed property partly because it was increasingly difficult to get new licences awarded. As a member of the Constitutional Association, Cain also had considerable influence on city politics. The fact that Cain himself remained popular, even when prohibition looked possible in the 1890s, suggests that he was just as astute at managing public opinion as he was at brewing beer.

---

30 Malcolm, *Anti-Booze Crusaders in Victorian Liverpool*, pp. 41–42.

4

King of the Toxteths

By the 1870s Liverpool was in many ways an affluent, elegant town. It had its own stock exchange and commodity markets, all the major banks had offices there and it was rivalled only by London as a centre for insurance. From Henry Tate's sugar importing and refining business which began in Liverpool in 1869, to Birkenhead shipbuilder Laird's, Liverpool's Victorian industrialists and entrepreneurs were among the most successful anywhere in the world. Liverpool's wealth and success was celebrated in its architecture. From St George's Hall plateau to the spires of Alfred Waterhouse's Lime Street Station Hotel and the stylish solidity of the financial buildings around Water Street and Castle Street, by the 1870s Liverpool had the appearance of a confident, powerful city. Even after the destruction caused by bombing in World War II and the insensitive redevelopment that took place almost throughout the twentieth century, Liverpool retains some of the finest Victorian architecture in the country.

In other areas, too, Liverpool was coming of age. In 1868 an Act of Parliament made Liverpool the first borough in Britain to be allowed to begin work on a tram system, while

the opening of the Walker Art Gallery in 1877 cemented
Liverpool's growing reputation as a centre for fine art and
the decorative arts and crafts. By 1880, when Liverpool was
finally granted city status, it was spreading out, expanding
into suburbs and taking on a more modern, Victorian
outlook.

Yet Liverpool's dark side remained. While public health
and housing were improving, in the 1870s and 1880s the
city was still blighted by widespread poverty and crime. In
particular, the 'cornermen' who hung around outside pubs
and extracted money from passers-by became one of Liverpool's most notorious groups. In his book *The Gangs of Liverpool*, Michael Macilwee recounts the story of the 'Tithebarn
Street outrage' in which Samuel Morgan was kicked to death
while walking home with his wife. The murder took place in
front of a crowd of onlookers who did nothing to help:

> These people lived as enemies of all authority. They instinc-
> tively sympathised with the ruffians and had become so used
> to violence that it no longer bothered them.
>   The press outrage stirred by Tithebarn Street ... was also
> a response to the atrocious behaviour of the crowd. Their
> inaction was only a symptom of something much larger and
> more frighteningly dangerous. Not only were the specta-
> tors judged to have been accomplices in the murder, but the
> whole community was viewed as morally corrupt.[31]

Perhaps even more disturbingly, the violent activities of
gangs who fought for territory, for pride, and in the name of
Irish sectarian causes took place no more than a few hundred
metres from the showy affluence of Dale Street and the
financial centre. While Liverpool attempted to grow into a

---

31 Michael Macilwee, *The Gangs of Liverpool: From the Cornermen to the High Rip,
the Mobs that Terrorised a City* (Wrea Green: Milo Books, 2006), pp. 80–81.

dignified Victorian city, a large section of the population still lived outside civilised society.

One of the problems this raised for Cain and his brewery was that much of the violence and crime was associated with pubs and drunkenness. In fact, pubs were one of the prime targets for criminal gangs looking for easy money as well as being the places where the cornermen gathered. Elsewhere, in cities such as Manchester or London, crime was also a serious problem, but Liverpool's reputation as a place of violence and moral degradation went ahead of them all. This atmosphere of violence and crime helped build support for temperance campaigners who saw drink as the cause of Liverpool's problems. As the temperance movement gathered momentum in the 1870s and later, brewers such as Cain in Toxteth, H. K. Aspinall in Birkenhead, and John Houlding in Everton all battled with increasingly powerful opposition to 'The Trade'.

Although best known for its shipping and financial industries, Liverpool was also a manufacturing city, and by 1886 it was confident enough in its commercial reputation to host the International Exhibition of Commerce, Navigation and Industry on a site at Wavertree. Opened by Queen Victoria on 11 May, the exhibition summed up in its title Liverpool's three areas of economic might. Civic pride spurred the city to build the Wavertree exhibition site on a grander scale than any similar exhibition London could muster, though it was dismissed outside Liverpool as the 'Shipperies'.

In the years leading up to 1870 the brewery on Stanhope Street had been transformed. This was the point when Cain's business developed from being a successful local brewery into a significant force in the local market. He owned many pubs and increased production relentlessly throughout the 1870s and 1880s. In 1887 he began a major programme of building at the brewery that would allow continuing expansion into the twentieth century and gave it a theoretical capacity of 400,000 barrels a year. It is this forward-thinking approach that lies behind Cain's success as an entrepreneur.

Both the success of the business and Cain's political influence can be explained in part by the spread of Liverpool itself but also by the way Cain adapted to changing social conditions. The 1870s were the decade in which Liverpool's growing population of skilled manual and white-collar workers began to move in large numbers outside the boundaries of the early nineteenth-century town. After 1870, when the Education Act forced local councils to provide schooling for all children under the age of 14, the supply of educated workers grew rapidly. This helped to sustain Liverpool's major firms through a period of growth that lasted into the twentieth century. But the extra money they earned also changed the city in other ways. The spread of the rail network charts the growth of the suburbs: Wavertree station opened in 1870, followed by Hunts Cross in 1874 and Aintree in 1880.

The consecration of churches at Old Swan, Mossley Hill, Allerton, Wavertree and elsewhere indicates where new residential areas were springing up in the 1870s. The construction of places of worship also shows how cosmopolitan Liverpool's population was becoming. The city's Jewish population had been large enough to warrant building a dedicated synagogue as far back as 1807, but by the 1870s, after decades of immigration from Northern Europe, the community played a significant part in Liverpool life. In

1871 the architects W. and G. Audsley won the competition to build what Joseph Sharples describes as 'one of the finest examples of Orientalism in British synagogue architecture'.[32] Opened in 1874, the highly decorated synagogue is located on Princes Road, near the junction with Stanhope Street. In a display of inter-faith tolerance that was rare in other parts of Liverpool at the time, the synagogue stands almost alongside the church of St Margaret, one of Liverpool's most important Anglo-Catholic churches. St Margaret's was itself built in 1868–1869 and paid for, as Sharples notes, by stockbroker Robert Horsfall. Just across the road on Berkley Street stands the Greek Orthodox church of St Nicholas, rounding out a group of religious buildings that reflected at least some of Liverpool's diversity. Built in Byzantine style with domes and round-arched windows, St Nicholas's opened in 1870.

As they moved out of the old overcrowded neighbourhoods, the seedy old-style beer houses and pubs were no longer places this new 'respectable' working-class population wanted to spend its money. The pubs that were built to service the new suburbs in the 1870s and 1880s were bigger and more comfortable; they were social places rather than drinking dens. The most celebrated pubs in Liverpool, The Vines and The Philharmonic Dining Rooms, would not be built for at least another two decades. But brewers such as Cain were beginning to respond to the needs of this new social group and to pressure from the magistrates' bench to reduce drunkenness and crime.

The general gradual improvement in the image of brewing and beer also extended to the brewery itself. Like

32 Joseph Sharples, *Liverpool* (Pevsner Architectural Guides) (New Haven and London: Yale University Press, 2004), p. 249.

many brewers, Cain took a fatherly approach to his workers, rewarding them with an annual outing, entering the brewery horses into competitions and displays, as well as other benefits. Some of the bigger brewers even offered subsidised clothing and shoes which they sold on the brewery premises. While they were not especially well paid, brewery workers were traditionally well looked after by their employers and were fiercely loyal. In fact many of those working at Cain's brewery during the 1940s and 1950s, when it was owned by Higson's, were second- or even third-generation brewery workers.

Cain's brewery, and the loyalty of his workers, made him a formidable political force. He allowed the Constitutional Association to use brewery vehicles and brewery employees for political campaigning, while horse-drawn drays carried voters to the polling stations and distributed pamphlets around Liverpool. By the 1880s he had become a powerful player in Liverpool's system of 'boss politics', a feature of government that singled it out from other towns.

Nineteenth-century Liverpool was increasingly run by a group of wealthy, influential men who dominated the city's social and political life. In *A History of the Corporation of Liverpool*, Brian D. White explains that 'of sixty-four members of the Council [in 1856] twenty-seven were merchants, brokers and shipowners'.[33] Of these, 19 were Tories and six were brewers or distillers. And while this was less than in 1835, the growing number of tradesmen on the council also tended to have Tory leanings. In more practical terms, while merchants gradually drifted away from formal politics, individual wards were increasingly controlled by

33 Brian D. White, *A History of the Corporation of Liverpool* (Liverpool: Liverpool University Press, 1951), p. 88.

'bosses' in much the same way as in American cities. White notes that in the 1850s the two Toxteth wards were controlled by the timber trade. But by the 1870s it was Robert Cain who had been crowned 'King of the Toxteths'.

Boss politics was built on the relationship between the wealthy merchant bosses and the large population of working poor. While the divide between rich and poor was marked right across Victorian Britain, in Liverpool it was perhaps more obvious than elsewhere. The distressing signs of deep and hopeless poverty were on show even in the stylish financial district. This dramatic contrast between the wealth of Liverpool's merchant families and the striking poverty of a large number of its citizens helped to focus power in the hands of a small number of business owners and the politicians who were loyal to them. Workers who did have jobs felt grateful to their bosses for raising them from the poverty they saw all around them.

There were several reasons why brewers were especially prominent in local Tory politics in the 1870s and 1880s. First there was the issue of licensing. Brewers and distillers had an interest in being supportive of the ruling political group since that way they could influence licensing policy. Secondly, the Liberal Party broadly supported the claims of temperance campaigners. It was enjoying a revival of fortunes as the better-off, Tory-voting population moved to the outer suburbs where there were fewer council seats. Thirdly, antagonism between brewing interests and the Liberal Party was spurred by the activities of the so-called Watch Committee, which as White explains, pressed the municipal police force to crack down on drunkenness in Liverpool's pubs:

The publicans at first protested strongly against this infringe-
ment of their liberties and the Watch Committee had some
difficulty in persuading them to co-operate with the police.
This may perhaps be regarded as the beginning of the conflict
which later became acute between the Liberal Party and the
liquor trade.[34]

Drunkenness had been a growing problem in Liverpool over
the previous decade, and in 1878 the Watch Committee even
went so far as to appoint a group of police officers specifically to the task of inspecting pubs.

At a time when the Tory Party in Liverpool had to work
harder to secure enough votes to protect its majority in the
council, employers such as Cain were highly prized. The
brewer's popularity among working-class drinkers in the
Toxteth wards also brought him influence in the party. By the
1880s it appears that Cain was a senior figure in the Constitutional Association, the political club in which battles over
policies and candidates were won and lost. Reporting on the
death of Robert Cain, the *Daily Post and Mercury* made a
point of highlighting his influence on local politics:

> In the Toxteths Mr. Cain was for many years looked upon as a
> powerful factor in elections, on the Conservative side, and his
> position earned for him the designation, years ago, of 'King
> of the Toxteths'. His influence never obtruded much into the
> public eye, and probably for this reason he was all the more
> valuable to his party, pulling the election strings behind the
> men who were publicly recognised as party leaders. ... He
> never himself took a personal part in any candidature, always
> declining to enter public life.[35]

Like most powerful merchants of the time, Cain avoided
running for office himself, but there were exceptions to

34 White, *Corporation of Liverpool*, p. 108.
35 *Daily Post and Mercury*, 20 July 1907.

the gradual withdrawal of merchants from front-line local politics. John Houlding, a brewer and acquaintance of Cain's, was one of these. Like Cain he was known as the 'King' of his local stamping ground, but he was also chairman of the Everton Conservative Association and chose to translate his popularity into votes. He was elected to represent Everton and Kirkdale wards in 1884 and became Mayor of Liverpool in 1897. Even so, much of the real power was located behind the scenes in the hands of wealthy men who did not themselves stand for election.

Liverpool's powerful merchants in the 1870s and 1880s presided over companies that were, on the whole, family owned. Sons followed fathers into the family firm in much the same way as the old aristocratic families had passed on titles and estates. Share issues were common as a way of raising money and Liverpool's own stock exchange did brisk business in the shares of shipping lines and insurance companies, making millionaires of many local brokers. But names such as Lever, Holt and Walker, which still resonate in the twenty-first-century city, confirm that the identity and ownership of most firms was tightly bound to their founding families. It is likely that this had a positive effect on Cain's political influence, since his personal popularity overcame any objections to his trade.

But there were drawbacks to running a family firm, not least of which was the issue of inheritance. Cain was among the merchants who successfully managed the handover of ownership to his sons, but even for him running a family firm was not without its problems. For one thing, the five sons competed with each other for influence at the brewery, sometimes employing dirty tricks to gain the upper hand. It was only after incorporation, when company minutes from the late 1890s reveal how the shares were divided, that clear favourites, headed by sons Charles and William, began to emerge.

As the company records after 1896 show, Cain provided for all of his children and their families long before his death through the allocation of shares. But the problem of finding a successor was something that had concerned him since the birth of his first son, Robert James Cain, in 1848. As the eldest son, Robert James stood to take over from his father as a matter of course. But unlike aristocratic families, where heredity overrules most other considerations, firms depend on the competence and commitment of their leaders. Robert James, whose various careers included 'builder' and 'concert agent', as well as 'master brewer', does not seem to have shown the qualities his father demanded.

In one family story Robert James was engaged in making sure the company's tenant publicans were keeping clean houses and serving well-kept beer. Being a man who liked a drink, young Robert gave in to temptation once too often. He was caught drunk in one of the pubs by his younger brothers, Charles and William, who told their father. This story of Robert James Cain falling out with his father seems to repeat Robert senior's own dispute with his father James. A story passed down to Robert James's descendants describes him being banished to sea for several years following this incident. This is almost certainly not what happened to Robert James, since the dates of birth of his children allow for only a short period of absence in the late 1880s, when he was 40 years old. More likely the subject of the story was Robert senior, years earlier, who was banished to work on the palm oil ships and from that point onwards all but broke off contact with his extended family.

Robert James Cain was difficult and headstrong from the start. By the late 1860s his father had a reputation and a social position to maintain and the two must have been at odds even then. For example, when Robert James married Sarah Turner in 1867 the wedding seems to have taken place away from his father's influence. On the marriage certificate he gives his place of residence as 67 Stanhope Street, the address of the brewery. Sarah Turner, who lived on Aigburth Road, was just 17 years old when the marriage took place. Her father was a carter and she was a woollen piecer, a skilled manual job usually done by children. That this young couple, whose social positions were so far apart, should have chosen to marry in Walton, far from their respective families, suggests they did so without the approval of their parents. Despite this poor start Robert and Sarah Cain made a success of their marriage and had ten or more children. One of their daughters, Ethel, became a professional singer and performed in concert halls around the country.

Some time after the death of his father James Cain in 1871, Robert Cain and his family moved to 'Barn Hey', a house he had built in three acres of land on Aigburth Road, not far from Sefton Park. This was a time when members of Liverpool's new merchant class were beginning to make their mark on the city by spending extravagant amounts of money on large houses surrounded by acres of land. The areas around Sefton Park, Mossley Hill and St Michaels became the most fashionable places to live, and by the 1890s the houses and extensive gardens they developed had become one of the most notable features of Liverpool. The Cain family's own three acres just off Aigburth Road was one of the smaller estates, but the house was among the most flamboyant in the area, built in high Victorian style with at least 12 bedrooms. The Cains must have been among the first wealthy families to move into the area, though 'Barn Hey' was outside the fashionable ring of large houses surrounding Sefton Park. But they would have been part of a social circle that included shipping line owners, industrialists and financiers, the emerging movers and shakers of Victorian Liverpool.

After the relative isolation of life in Grassendale Park, 'Barn Hey' must have seemed a busy place. By 1874, the year their eldest daughter Hannah died, aged 24, and their youngest, Gertrude, was born, the Cains had eight children under the age of 18, four of them under the age of 10. The house was only a short distance by horse-drawn omnibus from Stanhope Street and although he continued to work long hours at the brewery, Cain had more time to devote to other interests. It may be significant that Cain did not choose to live in the heart of the Sefton Park enclave. By the 1880s 'Barn Hey' was flanked by terraced housing inhabited by white-collar and skilled manual workers, the very people who bought Cain's beer and who voted for the Conservative Party candidates Cain supported. These were the people Cain later depended on to bring respectability to his pubs and to vote for policies that would favour brewing interests. As Cain's children grew up and bought houses of their own, many of them lived near to 'Barn Hey', including at the house next door, 'The Hollies'. Cain's reputation as 'King of the Toxteths' was no doubt bolstered by the closeness of his family and their visibility in the local area. The Cains were well known and well liked in the area between Sefton

Park and St Michael's Hamlet, where the family attended church.

Like other self-made men, Cain lacked a family history he could rely on to bring him automatic status and respect. The family he had left behind in the Scotland Road slums was by this time getting a modest living from making shoes, but their situation was precarious. The Irish population of Liverpool was held responsible for much of the violence and immoral behaviour for which the city was notorious. The size and imposing style of 'Barn Hey' on Aigburth Road was already a testament to what Cain had achieved in a little over two decades. He described it as a 'comfortable place on two or three acres of ground' but as his interviewer in the *Liverpool Review* put it 'some people would describe it differently'.[36] Certainly there could be no doubting the wealth and success of its owner.

But conspicuous displays of wealth were not enough to secure a place at the high table of Liverpool's elite families, and by the 1870s Cain was doing his best to make sure everybody knew that he was not only a rich man and a hardworking man, but also a man of culture and taste. The family embraced Victorian high culture in ways that would have seemed unimaginable to Cain's father thirty years earlier. One example of this is Cain's relationship with the painter William Daniels, a portrait artist whose work earned him the title of 'Liverpool Rembrandt' for the way it exploited contrast between light and shade. Daniels was born in 1813 and grew up in the brick fields of the Vauxhall area of Liverpool. Like Cain he was self-educated, and he had only limited training in drawing at the Royal Institution on Liverpool's

---

36 *Liverpool Review*, 17 September 1887, p. 10.

Colquitt Street. Unlike the brewer, Daniels was a wild and undisciplined man who drank too much and frequented some of Liverpool's most notorious neighbourhoods.

Daniels, who painted portraits of such notables as the engineer George Stephenson and had his work exhibited at the Kensington museums in London, was also known to paint pub signs to make ends meet. He was often commissioned to paint portraits of Liverpool's wealthy families and in the 1870s he became a favourite with the Cain family at 'Barn Hey'. He produced many paintings there, including at least two portraits of Cain himself. The *Liverpool Review* takes up the story:

> [Mr. Cain] is fortunate in being in possession of a large number of oil paintings by the celebrated Daniels. That dissolute and strangely independent genius worked for no man as he did for Mr. Cain, in whose house he spent many of his days and where his eccentric pride and sensibility were respected so as to avoid giving any chance of his throwing up the work or striking his brush through a picture which was a common incident with him.[37]

In Robert Cain's will three paintings by Daniels are mentioned specifically. One is entitled 'A boy selling matches' while the other two are portraits, large and small, of Cain himself. The larger of these portraits, painted in 1873, of a stern-looking Robert Cain in formal dress, a shock of dark curly hair and side whiskers, was used by the brewery in its advertising in the 1990s.

Fine art and music went alongside industry, shipping and trade as part of Liverpool's emergence as one of Victorian Britain's great cities. The industrialists whose wealth built

37 *Liverpool Review*, 17 September 1887, p. 10.

the great civic buildings and the vast houses and estates in what were then the outer suburbs acquired the tastes and culture that had once belonged almost exclusively to the established rural aristocracy. In becoming a patron and friend of the painter Daniels, and later G. Hall Neale, Cain was not only indulging a passion for art that would see him build a large collection of paintings over the following decades, but was also asserting his place in Britain's new hierarchy. Tony Lane explains how the families of entrepreneurs in the mid-nineteenth century came to be seen as Liverpool's aristocracy, leaving their names on streets and hospitals, museums and college buildings. Their wealth was immense:

> At its peak, in the years 1880–1899, Liverpool produced as many millionaires as Manchester, West Yorkshire, West Midlands, Tyneside and East Anglia combined. ... from 1804–1914, Merseyside produced almost twice as many millionaires as Greater Manchester and, outside London, was only surpassed by Clydeside.[38]

While the Cain family in 1880 was not in the same league in terms of wealth as the McIvers, who owned Cunard, the Ismays, who owned the White Star Line, or the Rathbones, a Liverpool 'Old Family' of long standing, these were the circles in which they were moving.

Liverpool's wealthy families lived lives of comfort and luxury that the vast majority of Liverpudlians could only dream about. They socialised together, formed trade organisations so that they could work together in their own interests, yet kept themselves apart from the town to which they

38 Tony Lane, *Liverpool: Gateway of Empire* (London: Lawrence and Wishart, 1987), p. 55.

owed their success. But they were also behind many of the improvements and enhancements to the emerging city and contributed a great deal to the lives of its citizens. In the case of Robert Cain this took the form of political activity and philanthropy. Cain was a popular figure in Liverpool by the late 1870s with a reputation not only as a firm but fair employer but also as a generous supporter of charities.

Unlike many of his fellow entrepreneurs, Cain's philanthropy was low key and often anonymously given. Despite the flamboyant lifestyle his family enjoyed, his enthusiasm for having his portrait painted, and the diamond tie pins he wore, Robert Cain was in many ways an austere man dedicated to his work. Cain's advertising depicts the brewer as Father Christmas riding a dray loaded with casks and raising a pint of frothing ale as he passes the grand façade of his brewery. But although he was a cheerful man who enjoyed being in company, Cain had little time for frivolity. He no doubt enjoyed his wealth, but he was well aware of the effort and hard work behind it. The knowledge that his brother and sister still struggled to make ends meet in the slums was also a reminder of how different life could have been.

Others were perhaps more confident in their position and could be more open about their generosity. Another brewer, the Mayor of Liverpool Andrew Barclay Walker, paid for the construction of the Walker Art Gallery to stage exhibitions of contemporary art and, in time, to acquire collections of its own. The Walker Art Gallery, which came to house the most important art collection outside London, further enhanced Liverpool's status as a city of art and culture. The gallery building itself, built in the cultural complex around

St George's Hall, was designed by Cornelius Sherlock and H. H. Vale. It was constructed between 1874 and 1877 and the foundation stone was laid by the Duke of Edinburgh. Sharples describes the gallery as 'More decorative than the Museum and Library, [but] it is still chastely Neoclassical for its date'.[39] The Walker soon housed many artworks of national importance and, in conjunction with the Lady Lever Gallery in Port Sunlight, it made Merseyside home to one of the finest collections of pre-Raphaelite painting in the world.

When it came to Liverpool's University College, founded in 1881, the city's merchants were no less willing to offer their money and their names to professorships and buildings. William Rathbone, a Liberal MP and one of the principal fundraisers for the college, went to his business and social contacts in turn and persuaded them to fund chairs and set up departments. Tony Lane explains:

> ... in 1885 William Rathbone once again acted as 'broker' for the establishment of a department of engineering at the university: he recruited John Brunner (chemical manufacturer), Alfred Holt, Thomas Ismay, and Thomas Harrison (shipowners), and Sir Andrew Walker (brewer).[40]

Lane goes on to observe that the 'named buildings and professorships [of Liverpool University] read like a social register ... of once well known Liverpool merchants, shipowners, landowners and manufacturers'.[41] A statue of William Rathbone was erected in Sefton Park and unveiled in 1877.

Apart from Andrew Walker, whose grand gestures attempted to improve the cultural and intellectual side of

39 Sharples, *Liverpool*, p. 63.
40 Lane, *Gateway to Empire*, p. 62.
41 Lane, *Gateway to Empire*, p. 70.

Liverpool, brewers tended to be more interested in entertainment than education. Brewer and Conservative politician John Houlding is also known as a key figure in the emergence of Liverpool's two great football teams, Everton FC and Liverpool FC. Everton had been founded by St Domingo's Methodist Youth Club as St Domingo's FC in 1878, but was unable to find a permanent field on which to play until 1884. Houlding helped them strike a deal with yet another brewer, John Orrell, who owned a field off Anfield Road. Houlding became a leaseholder of the ground and spent a great deal of money on the club. But when he bought the land outright in 1891 he raised the rent, forcing Everton to move to Goodison Park. Meanwhile, with a field and no players, Houlding and Orrell formed Liverpool FC at Anfield. The two teams have been fierce rivals ever since, playing in the top flight of English football for most of their history.

The 1870s saw Liverpool develop as a cultural centre and as a place of trade and manufacturing. By the end of the decade it had an established and growing horse-drawn tram system, a developing railway network and expanding suburbs. George's landing stage, opened on 27 July 1874 and destroyed by fire the next day, was rebuilt a second time at a cost of £250,000 and reopened in April 1876, greatly expanding the capacity of the docks. In 1880 Liverpool became a diocese of the Church of England under Bishop Ryle and at the same time gained official city status.

By then the Cains were one of Liverpool's established families and in 1887 Robert Cain was an important enough figure to be profiled in the *Liverpool Review*, one of the city's most respected liberal journals. The front page of the 17

September issue features a line drawing of Cain in formal dress, with a heavy, wide-lapelled topcoat and fine waistcoat over a white shirt, his chest puffed out and his shoulders turned to one side. His curly hair is receding and he carries a full beard that reaches down to his shirt front. He looks out of the page with stern authority, his eyes clear and his brow clenched in a serious frown. He is the model of a Victorian industrialist. Beneath the picture is a caption: '"Let the end try the man" – Shakspere'. Robert Cain was more than capable of holding his own with the city's most powerful leaders and counted many of them among his friends. Yet the family's circle of acquaintances went much wider than the merchant elite into which they had so recently been accepted. It reflected their own rapid rise from poverty to great wealth and also Liverpool's position as a global city.

On the night of the 1881 census, besides Robert, Ann, six of their children and three female servants, a young woman named Eliza A. Malvern was a visitor at 'Barn Hey'. She had been born on the Pacific island of Fiji 31 years earlier and usually lived in Beaumont Street, Toxteth, with her parents John and Fanny and her five grown-up brothers and sisters, the youngest of whom, Harry, was 18 years old. Eliza's father was a Wesleyan minister and Supernumary of the Grove Street Circuit. Years earlier, from the mid-1840s to the late 1850s, John Malvern and his family had lived in Fiji and Tonga in the South Pacific, where they were among the earliest missionaries in the islands. At that time missionary work in the region was highly dangerous. The native people did not embrace Christianity as readily as had been hoped and many missionaries were killed. Cannibalism was not unknown. John Malvern, who was about the same age as Robert Cain, managed to raise four children there and returned to England around 1859 where he took up a position as minister at the Wesley Methodist Church in Middleham, North Yorkshire.

Eliza's story demonstrates how the Cains retained contact with social spheres outside their own and also says something about their generosity. Almost a century before passenger aircraft made long-distance travel a common experience it is also an indication of how well-travelled Liverpool's inhabitants could be. As Wesleyan Methodists, the Malverns may even have been connected with the temperance movement, yet Eliza seems to have become a close acquaintance and a recipient of the family's kindness. A decade later she appears again in the Cain family census return, this time in the position of 'ladies' companion'. A step above a common servant, Eliza kept Ann Cain company in exchange for her board and lodging and a small allowance. For a single woman in her forties with no money of her own this was probably the best she could hope for.

Eliza was lucky to have found a position of comfort and security when so many others were being left behind, and her story is just one of several that reflect well on Ann Cain in particular. Ann was probably responsible for maintaining contact between her husband and his extended family in Liverpool, especially when the relationship became easier after the death of his father. She seems to have used her influence over her husband to help find work for his nephews and nieces.

As the 1880s began Liverpool resumed its frantic growth after the slowdown of the 1870s. With city status newly conferred, Liverpool entered a gilded age which lasted a little over thirty years. This was to be the era of the 'merchant princes', of the great steamships, and seemingly limitless technological advances. For Robert Cain and his brewery it was a period of expansion and growth and was crowned at the end of the century by the building of his new mansion at Hoylake, the 'terracotta palace' addition to the brewery, and his own 'Three Graces': The Central Hotel, The Vines and The Philharmonic Dining Rooms.

5

The Gilded Age

By the year of Robert Cain's death in 1907 the Mersey Brewery had spread well beyond its original Stanhope Street site. The two major additions that Cain had made in the 1880s and 1890s were still hemmed in by the flour mills that stood between Britton Street and Parliament Street. But across Stanhope Street the Harrington Elementary School found itself a close neighbour to the massive brewery stables and must have been a distracting place to learn to read and write. To the rear, across Mann Street, were the bonded stores, the bottling stores and the cooperage. From its quite modest beginnings the Mersey Brewery had become one of the largest industrial complexes in the area. Putting all the sites together, it covered an area larger than the nearby Royal Southern Hospital, which opened on its new Hill Street site in 1872, and was almost as big as the Brunswick Goods Station alongside Toxteth Dock.

The period between 1880 and the beginning of the First World War was a gilded age in Liverpool and this was when the brewery saw its most dramatic developments. In 1887 Cain began a three-year building programme to expand the site, erecting a new building with a frontage on Stanhope Street that borrowed from Classical and Gothic styles. Architect James Redford designed the building and with its roofline finished off with decorative urns the new brewery was at the height of Victorian architectural fashion. The design incorporated parts of the old 1838 Hindley brewhouse and one part of it faced gable-end on to the street, looking for all the world like the end wall of a church. The gazelle motif and the Latin 'Pacem Amo' (I love peace) over the yard entrance made it clear that this cathedral of ale aimed to unify Liverpool's turbulent streets.

At the same time as building work was underway at the brewery, the area around it also saw significant redevelopment. In the early 1880s the crumbling housing immediately to the south of the main brewery site was a reminder of old Liverpool. Sanitation was almost non-existent and nearby housing had a history of diseases such as typhus and tuberculosis. In fact, the area around Mann Street and Upper Mann Street, which then ran unbroken from directly opposite the Mersey Brewery to an intersection with Park Road, was one of the most disease-ridden areas of Liverpool. Following the construction of St Martin's Cottages in 1869 there was a mood of optimism about housing reform in Liverpool. Several schemes were set up to pull down housing considered 'insanitary', but for the next decade or more the corporation did almost nothing to replace them. On the whole the council preferred private builders to provide improved rented housing for the working poor and they tended to have their own interests at heart.

Then in 1882 a rise in the number of deaths from 'fever' led to a report on the state of Liverpool's housing and a change in the rules governing slum clearance. The council was given new powers under its leader Sir Arthur Forwood to demolish poor housing and the Insanitary Property Committee was set up to survey the city's housing. Brian D. White explains:

> It was estimated that there were at the time about 15,000 insanitary houses in the city. The cost of acquiring the sites of these and demolishing them was put at £750,000 and the cost of erecting new dwellings to rehouse two-thirds of the existing inhabitants of the insanitary houses was £660,000 ... it was thought that this would not involve an annual charge above a penny rate on the existing rateable value.[42]

Unfortunately the plan did not increase either the rate of demolition or the rehousing of the poor. Even when slums were cleared, the council's insistence on allowing private firms to redevelop the demolition sites meant that many of the displaced people could not afford the rents on the new properties. They simply moved to another slum.

Despite the slow rate of progress, by 1907 slum clearances had swept away most of the worst housing in the area around the brewery. It was replaced with neat 'Welsh' terraces of six-room houses with proper sewers and small back yards. By 1900 even Liverpool Corporation was beginning to develop housing of its own in significant numbers. It also put a great deal of effort into the design and quality of its new housing stock so that 'By 1914 Liverpool had become something of a show-place from this point of view, and the Corporation was commended for the standard of its housing from abroad as well as from England'.[43]

It was also during the 1880s that the Mersey Brewery became a truly family concern. In the 1870s Cain's eldest son, Robert James, lived with his wife Sarah at 65 Stanhope

---

42 White, *Corporation of Liverpool*, p. 134.
43 White, *Corporation of Liverpool*, p. 138.

Street, right next door to the brewery, and by 1880 he had given up his career as a builder and was working as a brewer in the family firm. It was not to last and within a few years Robert James moved to the Channel Islands to live on his 'independent means'. By then it was becoming clear that the other sons, Alfred, William, Charles and Herbert, would be more willing to work together. Cain's daughters were mostly excluded from involvement in running the business.

Alfred, William, Charles and Herbert all listed their profession as 'brewer' in the 1890s. The family also had connections by marriage with another brewer, Shaw's of Ashton under Lyne. Both Alfred Cain and his sister, Lena, married members of the Shaw family, and after Alfred's death in 1899 his wife, Mary, was represented at Robert Cain and Sons board meetings by her brother, George. Lena, who married Henry Shaw in 1886, lived with him near the Dukinfield Brewery in Ashton. They moved with their children to Hoylake in the late 1890s.

The increasing size of Cain's brewing operation in the 1880s, and the redevelopment of the brewery itself, meant that by the 1890s the brewery was one of the most advanced in the country. The Cain family was also spreading out into the area around the family home and 'Barn Hey' became the hub for family social occasions, which would have included musical entertainments and lavish dinner parties. By the early 1890s most of Robert and Ann Cain's children lived in large houses nearby. Alfred lived with his wife and children next door at 'The Hollies' while William, who married Florence Roberts in 1886, lived a few minutes' walk away at 15 Ivanhoe Road. Charles and his wife Florence Nall, whom he married in 1888, were also living in Toxteth Park. By this time the brewery was doing well enough to support several families, all of them living in large, opulent mansions in one of the most desirable parts of Liverpool. It was a comfortable and satisfying life.

Part of the reason for the increasing success of the brewery and brewing in general in the 1880s was the election of William Gladstone as Prime Minister in 1880. The British economy had suffered a slump in the early 1870s which was coupled with political troubles for Gladstone's Liberal government. In 1874 Disraeli's Conservatives took power and a year later, as the depression in farming reached its lowest point, bought shares in the Suez Canal to give Britain control of the important trade route. By 1876, when Queen Victoria became Empress of India, conditions at home were beginning to improve, but trade was still weak and defeats for the British Army in Africa did nothing for morale. By 1880 the country was ready for a change and Gladstone's Liberal Party took power again. For brewers, Gladstone's return to government was highly significant.

The link between brewing and government is a long-established one. Successive governments in the nineteenth century tinkered with the way brewing was taxed and regulated, but there had been no attempt to undo Wellington's Beer Act of 1830. After the Beer Act, brewers were taxed on the ingredients they used to the point that, after the cost of malt and hops, excise duty was the brewer's third largest expense. From the mid-1850s the duty on malt, sugars and hops was gradually reduced and in 1863 the ailing English hop farms were boosted by the abolition of duty on hops, though competition from Germany and the United States continued to cause problems. Cain's brewery, for example, was using Bavarian hops in the 1860s.

One of Gladstone's first actions as Prime Minister in 1880 was to remove all duty on malt and the other raw materials of beer and put it on the finished product. This was partly in response to the temperance movement. Applying duty to beer allowed the government to control the price and the alcoholic content more directly. By increasing the duty, the government not only pushed up the price of beer, but also encouraged brewers to reduce the alcohol, since weaker beer could be sold at a lower price. For brewers, who complained about the government's attempt to control the market, the benefit came in the form of lower prices for raw materials and an increase in profits. But it tended to be the larger brewers, who could demand the lowest prices, who did best of all. Conditions for brewers in the 1880s and 1890s forced many small brewers out of business; many were bought by larger concerns.

Just as he was lucky to have begun brewing while the market was still open to small brewers, by the 1890s Cain's brewery was large enough to be one of the survivors. In 1880 Liverpool had 70 common brewers producing more than 10,000 barrels of beer each year. That figure had almost halved by 1890 and stood at just 28 in 1900. In the same period the number of licensed victuallers, who sold beer to the public, was almost unchanged at around 2,300.[44] After 1880 larger brewers like Cain's rapidly increased their share of the market, buying out smaller brewers and taking over their pubs and licences. This was partly in response to a sharp reduction in the number of new licences available. But an additional incentive was that, as slum clearance began at last

44 Gourvish and Wilson, *The British Brewing Industry*, pp. 70–71.

to make an impact on Liverpool's housing stocks, brewers were compensated for the loss of pubs, often at above the market value of the buildings themselves.

Although he welcomed his sons into the business, Robert Cain was careful to retain control for himself almost up to the last. He put in regular and demanding hours at the brewery until a few months before his death, but in the 1890s he seems to have been aware of the need to prepare the brewery and the family for life after he had gone. As one of the city's wealthiest and most influential families, the Cains lived in great luxury. Little more than a decade after it was invented they used telephones to talk to one another and Robert Cain himself had two numbers, one at home and one at the brewery. Their houses were filled with paintings, fine porcelain, original art works and ornately carved furniture. And while theirs was 'new' money, the Cains surrounded themselves with the trappings of 'old' wealth. They had a lot to lose and Robert Cain had a clear memory of what having nothing was like.

Perhaps it was the death of his wife Ann on 12 March 1896 that made up Robert Cain's mind to convert the brewery into a limited company. Although he had done well running it as a privately owned business, incorporation had the advantage of separating the company's assets and debts from those of its owners. The new company was known as Robert Cain and Sons Ltd, a limited liability company that made its shareholders responsible for any debts, but only up to the amount left unpaid on their shares. As in most cases, the liability was non-existent, since Cain allocated shares 'fully paid' to his sons and daughters. But in any case the brewery was also a highly profitable and secure business, with a great deal of property around Liverpool. Besides 'Cain's Superior Ales and Stouts' advertised on billboards and pub frontages across the city, the company also supplied its pubs with whisky and other imported drinks.

The allocation of shares allowed Cain to give his children a stake in the business and to manage his succession more easily. The new company was registered on 11 December 1896 and the first meeting was held ten days later with Alfred Dean Cain in the chair. His brothers, William, Charles and Herbert, made up the other three directors and W. Watson Rutherford, who had acted as Cain's solicitor for many years, was also present. The business was valued at £1 million and the shares were worth £10 each. Robert Cain, who took the role of chairman, held 50,000 ordinary shares and 49,994 'preference shares'. Preference shares give their holder privileges of some kind, such as the right to be part of the decision making, and this seems to have been the case here. Cain's children, Alfred, William, Charles, Herbert, Lena and Gertrude, each received a single preference share, leaving the founder with complete control of the company. For a while Lena and Gertrude attended board meetings, but it must have become clear that it was the men who were going to take control of the company and they drifted away. Notably absent from the list of shareholders are Robert James Cain, who by this time was enjoying life at his estate 'Fauvic', near St Helier, Jersey, and Sarah Ann Cain, by then married to John Howard and living in an apartment in the same house as her brother, Charles.

Over the coming months and years Robert Cain transferred preference shares to his sons, giving them increasing influence over the running of the business while retaining a tight grip on it for himself. He also began to transfer property to the business, reducing the size of his personal estate. On 9 April 1902, for example, the board met to consider 'the free transfer of the following properties' to the company: 'The Hollies', Aigburth Road, 'Barn Hey', Aigburth Road, three adjoining terraced houses on Upper Parliament Street, and a further house on Aigburth Road named 'South Grange', tenanted by a Dr McDougal. Also part of this transfer were 'two houses, land, and property, on Marine Parade, Hoylake'.

Both 'Barn Hey' and 'The Hollies' were sold three years later to J. H. and D. J. Roberts, while Cain paid the company £1 per year in rental for the property on Marine Parade, as well as the gardener's cottage and the stables of his new house, also called 'Barn Hey', at Hoylake. Cain's efforts to reduce the size of his personal estate by converting it into company assets which he controlled as the principal share-holder show an astute and tough-minded businessman at work. At the same April meeting in which he handed over the properties Cain persuaded the board to sign an agree-ment not to sell or transfer their shares; he on the other hand remained free to transfer shares to members of the family. Cain was determined to make sure that control over the brewery was transferred in exactly the way he decided, and although by this time his signature was shaky, he managed his sons' accession with a firm hand.

In the late 1890s the Cain family moved almost as one away from the expanding urban sprawl of Toxteth to new estates they had built on the other side of the Mersey, near Hoylake. This was the time in which Liverpool's merchant elite were at the height of their power and influence. Like their counterparts in New York, whose privileged lives are described by writers such as Henry James and Edith Wharton, Liverpool's wealthy merchants built houses and estates on a grand scale. T. H. Ismay's 'Dawpool' was among the largest of these. Built in 1896 to a design by Richard Norman Shaw, 'Dawpool' stood near the beach and cliffs at Thurstaston on Wirral. It was a vast mock-Jacobean mansion with massive chimneys and an imposing frontage. The scale of the building is difficult to appreciate, but Joseph Sharples notes in *Merchant Palaces* that when the house was demolished in 1927 one of the fireplaces was so large that it found a new life as the entrance to a restaurant in Birkenhead.

Such houses were a step beyond the earlier mansions built around Sefton Park. Both 'The Hollies' and 'Barn Hey' on Aigburth Road were substantial properties in their own right, but the new house Cain built among the dunes of Hoylake, and nearby 'Wilton Grange', built by his son William in 1905, were on an altogether different scale. All that remains of Robert Cain's mansion are its magnificent gateposts, still clearly visible on Meols Drive. Like other houses of its kind it was demolished for redevelopment in the twentieth century and the land on which it stood is now occupied by an estate of smaller modern homes. When they were built, such grand houses reflected the family's desire to join the ranks of the established aristocracy. But they were also new, modern buildings, fitted out with the latest luxuries. Thomas Edison brought electric light to the houses of New York City's wealthy families in the early 1880s and by the 1890s Liverpool's richest merchants were enjoying it too.

In common with many Liverpool mansions, 'Wilton Grange' was photographed by Bedford Lemere and features

in Sharples's *Merchant Palaces*. An image of the landing illus-
trates the world that Liverpool's merchants inhabited.[45] On
the one hand, William Cain's house is furnished in baronial
style with a decorative suit of armour, gilt-framed paintings,
and 'seventeenth-century' furniture. A bust of his father
Robert glowers from the top of the stairs. But on the other,
the tell-tale switches by a bedroom door and the absence of
heavy gas pipes in the ceiling lights reveal this as a modern
building with state-of-the-art fixtures and fittings.

One of the effects of moving away from Liverpool itself
was that it separated the Cains from their customers. Robert
Cain had made a name for himself in part because he lived
among the people he hoped to influence. But Liverpool's
merchants were not entirely isolated in their modern stately
homes. One of the reasons it had become possible for men
like Cain to live so far from their places of work was the
development of the city's transport network. In the 1860s
Cain had travelled on horseback from his home in Grassendale Park to the brewery. By the 1890s Liverpool's transport network was well developed, with horse-drawn trams
and omnibuses serving the suburbs, the Mersey Railway's
network spreading out beyond Aintree, and the Overhead
Railway or 'dockers' umbrella' running almost the full length
of the docks. The first electric tram service in Liverpool
began operation between Dingle and South Castle Street in
1898 and the service soon spread around the city.

It had also become much easier to cross the Mersey since
the opening of the railway tunnel in 1885. Before then the
only way to travel between Birkenhead and Liverpool was

---

45 Joseph Sharples, *Merchant Palaces: Liverpool and Wirral Mansions Photographed by Bedford Lemere and Co.* (Liverpool: Bluecoat Press, 2007), plate 43.

by boat. Some hardy souls (including Nathaniel Hawthorne, who travelled to his work at the American Consulate from Rock Ferry during the 1850s) commuted to Liverpool this way and lived in Birkenhead and along the bank of the Mersey on the Wirral side. But the introduction of the railway tunnel meant that commuters could live further from the city. The Mersey tunnel was one of the great engineering feats of the Victorian age and quickly became a symbol of what Liverpool ingenuity could do when combined with the city's vast wealth. The mayors of Liverpool and Birkenhead shook hands in the middle on 12 February 1885, after four years of construction work, and the tunnel was declared open by the Prince of Wales in January 1886. The tunnel was a project that benefited everyone. Liverpool's Victorian elite, including Robert Cain himself, mingled with ordinary commuters on the platform and on the trains themselves.

While it could be said that the retreat of Liverpool's wealthiest citizens to the security of distant private estates was a turning away from their Liverpool roots, the 'gilded age' also changed the city itself. As the first big wave of slum clearances started to have an effect, Liverpool began to move away from the darker side of its rush to wealth and power. By the turn of the century the city's major buildings reflected its importance in the world. The 1880s had seen the construction of buildings such as the Victoria Building (1889–1892) which was the main building of University College, Liverpool, sometimes claimed as the original 'redbrick' university, and the Royal Infirmary (1887–1890) on Pembroke Place, both by architect Alfred Waterhouse. In the 1890s the central streets of the city were augmented by the bulk of the White Star Line offices on James Street

(1895–1898) and numerous new bank buildings, including the Adelphi Bank (1891–1892), Leyland and Bullin's Bank (1895) and Parr's Bank (1898–1901). Sharples notes that with the completion of Parr's Bank, 'Castle Street's C19 transformation was complete, making it one of the most opulent Victorian commercial streets in the country'.[46] Proper drainage and sewerage systems had also cleaned up the city. It had come a long way from the days when Nathaniel Hawthorne could complain about the 'ordinary mud of Liverpool'.

While travel around Liverpool had become easier and more comfortable, the shipping leaving the port was also very different from what it had been fifty years earlier. By the 1890s sail was quickly disappearing and the great steamships began to dominate the Mersey with their size, speed and glamour. Competition for the coveted Blue Riband, awarded to the ship with the fastest Atlantic crossing, pushed the shipping companies to build ships for speed as well as comfort. Liners such as Cunard's *Campania* (twice the holder of the Blue Riband in 1893 and 1894, and later converted into the world's first aircraft carrier during the First World War), *Lucania*, a three-time Blue Riband holder, and White Star's *Germanic* made regular sailings to New York and Boston. After 1900, as liners became larger, faster and more luxurious, Liverpool hosted great ships such as White Star Line's *Celtic*, the largest steamer afloat in 1901, as well as *Mauretania* and *Lusitania*, the largest and fastest ships of the Edwardian age. *Mauretania* was converted to a troopship in 1915 while berthed in the Gladstone Dock.

The atmosphere of optimism and energy in Liverpool in the 1890s must have been infectious. As each new

46 Sharples, *Liverpool*, p. 26.

architectural and engineering marvel began to take shape Liverpudlians might have been forgiven for thinking they were witnessing a complete rebuilding of their city. Banks, shipping lines and insurance companies competed to build the grandest, most prestigious new building in Liverpool, and Robert Cain and his sons were keen to join in the frenzy. Pressure from the temperance campaigners, who by then had great influence on the magistrates' bench, forced brewers to respond to complaints that their pubs were dirty, unpleasant, immoral places. The tastes of the population were changing too and the city centre, with its art galleries, concert halls and theatres, was being transformed into a place where the new middle classes spent their after-work hours. As Liverpool grew richer, parts of the city were becoming more comfortable and more genteel. And while old-style pubs and beer houses continued to do good business, Cain knew he had to distance himself from the tough, violent image of the old Liverpool of his childhood.

In 1887, at the same time as the brewery itself was being rebuilt, Cain had undertaken a radical rebuilding of the old Albion public house in the middle of town. It was renamed the Central Commercial Hotel when the Central Station opened, a new ornate facade was erected on the front of the building and a small tower added to the roof, perhaps in tribute to Alfred Waterhouse's huge Lime Street Station Hotel of 1871. The façade carries the dates 1887, when Cain's renovation was completed, and 1675, a date for which there is no explanation. Apart from his beer, Cain's distinctive pubs were his legacy to the city and the Central was the first of three pubs that might justifiably be called his 'Three Graces'. By the late 1890s Cain shared the decision making at the brewery with his sons and no doubt they were influential in building two of Liverpool's most celebrated pubs, the Philharmonic Hotel and Dining Rooms and the Vines.

The Philharmonic, or 'The Phil' as it is known, is one of the city's architectural gems. On 29 December 1898 the board of the newly formed Robert Cain and Sons approved the contract for rebuilding the Philharmonic Hotel on the corner of Hardman Street and Hope Street. The cost was to be £12,450, a huge sum for the time and almost certainly not economic on its own terms. The 'fitting up', including the magnificent mahogany bar and partition walls, the mosaic floor and the glorious Art Nouveau lighting, was approved the following year, with the contract being awarded to Robert Garrett and Sons.

Designed by Walter W. Thomas, the new Philharmonic Hotel and Dining Rooms featured work by some of Liverpool's most skilled craftsmen. Painter G. Hall Neale, a close friend of Robert Cain, and his colleague Arthur Stratton from the School of Architecture and Applied Arts at the nearby University College, supervised the craftsmen. Sharples describes the richness of the interior:

> Repoussé copper panels by [H. Bloomfield] Bare are set in panelling on either side of the fireplace. More panels by Bare and Thomas Huson in the former billiard room; also plasterwork by C. J. Allen – a frieze and two figure groups, The Murmur of the Sea (over the fireplace) and attendants crowning a bust of Apollo (over the door).[47]

This description reads like a 'Who's Who' of Liverpool's flourishing arts and crafts community. The quality of the interior, and of the domed and gabled exterior, give a hint at

47 Sharples, *Liverpool*, p. 234.

the luxury and quality of Cain's own Hoylake residence but also of the great ships whose interiors were designed and built by many of the same craftsmen. Rounded off with magnificent wrought iron Art Nouveau gates, the Philharmonic is arguably Cain's great gift to the city, but its crowning glory is its gents lavatory. In a city that prides itself on its clear-headed realism and back-handed wit, male drinkers pass comment on the pretentiousness of their surroundings in the most lavishly appointed pub urinals in Britain. With a suitable chaperone, women are encouraged to take a look at the marble and the mahogany.

The Grade One listed Philharmonic is one of the country's finest public examples of Edwardian style and craftsmanship, but more importantly it quickly became one of Liverpool's favourite pubs and a standard bearer for what was known as the 'Improved Public House' movement. Popular with workers looking for supper and a beer after a hard day and with concertgoers and musicians spilling out of the Philharmonic Hall across the street, the Philharmonic was partly a response to the declining popularity of drinking in pubs in the 1890s. Because it was so near to the concert hall and the university, the Philharmonic was always a place where artists and musicians mingled with the general public. By the 1960s the area around Hope Street had become Liverpool's arts quarter, known simply by its postcode, 'Liverpool 8'. In his autobiography, *Said and Done*, poet and broadcaster Roger McGough describes how in the mid-1960s the Philharmonic became his favourite pub and emphasises the mix of people there:

> With its crystal chandeliers, copper panels, and ornate wooden friezes carved by craftsmen who had worked on the

> Cunard liners, it remains a magnificent symbol of Edwardian flamboyance. Most evenings ... I would meet up there with a group of teachers and artists, plumbers and sparks including my new pal John Gorman, and John Hewson, known as 'Hewo', the pub jester ...[48]

But the mixing of artists, performers and their audience has not always been a good thing. John Lennon complained that the worst thing about being famous was not being able to have 'a quiet drink in the Phil'.

The Philharmonic's position near to the university, in among the elegant Georgian housing off Hope Street and around Abercromby Square, gave it a comfortable, relaxed atmosphere in 1900. It was a world away from the squalid drinking dens and beer houses of Robert Cain's 'North End' childhood. But the interior quality and style of the Philharmonic was not reserved for Cain's customers in the middle-class areas of town. Not far away in terms of distance, but in a distinctly more urban setting, is the third of Cain's landmark pubs, the Vines. Completed in 1907, the 'riotously baroque'[49] pub was also designed by Walter W. Thomas, by then practically Cain's in-house architect. Sharples notes that most of the original cut-glass windows have been replaced with etched copies, presumably in the aftermath of wartime bombing, but the interior is every bit as lavish as the Philharmonic. Like the Philharmonic, the Vines was decorated by craftsmen of the highest quality. Sharples notes 'sumptuous fittings [which] include plaster reliefs by the Bromsgrove Guild and Gustave Hiller;[50] other features include beaten copper fireplaces and mahogany furniture.

48 Roger McGough, *Said and Done* (London, Century, 2005), p. 126.
49 Sharples, *Liverpool*, p. 184.
50 Sharples, *Liverpool*, p. 184.

The Vines is most striking on the outside. It is a building in tune with the excess and power of early twentieth-century Liverpool. Its flamboyant Dutch gables are out of scale with the rest of the building and it sports a clock big enough to be seen from almost anywhere on Lime Street. Built towards the end of the Edwardian period and finished in the year of Cain's death, the Vines is one of the last great flourishes of Liverpool's gilded age. Just like the better known 'Three Graces' at Pier Head, Cain's three landmark pubs represent the city's optimism and outward-looking vision in the years leading up to the First World War.

Reflecting on Robert Cain's life after his death in 1907, the *Liverpool Courier* said of the pubs:

> ... many of these [hostelries], in recent years, [have] at considerable expenditure, been reconstructed in such a way as to add them to the attractive structures of the city from an architectural point of view.[51]

Writing in *The Independent* in 1991, Michael Jackson said of the city's pubs that 'with flourishes of Queen Anne, art nouveau and neo-Renaissance design, no other city can match Liverpool by mile in the architecture of alcohol'.[52] That the street-level pubs should be so flamboyant and the Pier Head three so stately, elegant and, in the case of the Liver Building, so modern says a great deal about Liverpool itself. It is a city of enormous and serious influence around the world, but driven by an infectious sense of enthusiasm and light-heartedness. The spirit of Liverpool is as much in its street life as in the grand buildings that proclaim the city's global importance.

51 *Liverpool Courier*, 20 July 1907.
52 Michael Jackson, 'Reincarnation of the Real Brewers', *The Independent*, 6 July 1991.

The quality of the design and decoration of Cain's pubs was a celebration of Liverpool and the skills and tastes of its citizens. The brewer applied a similar sense of quality and care to the brewery building itself. After the remodelling of 1887–1890 the brewery was larger, more modern and more efficient than it had ever been in a century or more of operation. But by 1900 further work was needed to cope with increasing demand for Cain's quality ales. The brewery still in use in the twenty-first century was designed and built not only as a modern manufacturing plant, but as a landmark building. Now dwarfed by the Anglican Cathedral, in 1902 when the redbrick addition was completed the brewery must have been one of the tallest buildings in Toxteth, visible easily from across the river. And the detailing in the terracotta tilework, which carries the Cain's gazelle motif along with the founder's initials, is not limited to the outside faces of the building. Even in the delivery yard, high up on the walls where nobody ever looks, the 'XXXXX' symbol is on display. The Dusanj brothers, owners of the brewery since 2002, and great admirers of the building and its original owner, believe this to be a mark of Cain's attention to detail and quality. After all, even in the most out of the way places 'God can see it'.

In twenty-first-century Britain most industrial buildings are variations on a similar theme. Cost, rather than beauty, is the main influence on their design. The result is that, while most modern factories are highly efficient, very few could be described as interesting to look at. For Victorian industrialists, however, the factory and the warehouse were part of the cities in which they stood and an expression of their owners' wealth and influence. Perhaps because quality

ales are so closely tied to their place of origin, brewery buildings often feature in advertising for beer. Images of Robert
Cain's Mersey Brewery appeared on labels and company
stationery and the same was true of the Walker brewery in
Warrington and many others. Norman Cook, in his book
about Higson's, the firm that operated Cain's brewery for
most of the twentieth century, has this to say about the
building:

> Cain's brewery was, and still is, a magnificent example of
> Victorian architecture. It was developed painstakingly and
> lovingly by Robert Cain over the last half of the nineteenth
> century. It had a planned capacity of 400,000 barrels a year,
> but it could never have achieved more than half this output
> because of a lack of storage space for the raw materials
> and casks, and a ridiculously small yard through which all
> the raw materials, waste products, and full casks had to be
> handled.[53]

Brewery buildings such as Cain's were a celebration of
industry and sent out a powerful message to their customers,
telling them that here was a company where quality and
attention to detail took priority. Flamboyant tilework and
wasteful decoration were an indication of the company's
wealth and success. But they were also the mark of a company
that could be trusted not to cut corners on quality for the
sake of saving money.

   Though Robert Cain could not have known it, this
was the beginning of the final phase in the Cain family's
involvement with the brewery. Within two decades of the
completion of the 1902 brewery extension Robert Cain and
Sons would be taken over by Walker's of Warrington and

53 Norman Cook, *Higson's Brewery, 1780–1980* (Liverpool: Kershaw Press
Services, 1980), p. 30.

the brewery sold to Higson's, another well-known Liverpool brewer. By the time of Queen Victoria's death on 22 January 1901, Cain himself was 75 years old. And while he continued as an active chairman of the company beyond his eightieth birthday, he increasingly left the day-to-day running of the business to his sons, Charles, William and Herbert. In the course of his life Robert Cain had seen great changes. He had experienced life in some of Liverpool's worst and most overcrowded slums, but now found himself living in a large mansion with acres of land. He had seen the city transform itself from a grim, overcrowded place with a reputation as a slave trade port, to one where art and culture sat happily with industry, trade and commerce. As John Belchem argues in *Merseypride*, it continued to look outwards rather than to the rest of the country and while its attitude towards foreign countries may have been colonial, it was also open to foreign influence and ambition.

At the time of the coronation of King Edward VII in August 1902, Liverpool was in its pomp. It had a world-class art gallery and civic architecture the envy of every city outside London. Its university already boasted a celebrated medical faculty, including from 1898 the world's first School of Tropical Medicine, and was famous for its school of art. It had a modern transport system, with electric trams, and a well-developed rail network. At the dawn of the Edwardian era Liverpool's view of itself was optimistic. In the course of the next few years many of the city's most famous buildings were begun or finished. Construction work on the great Anglican Cathedral, designed by Sir Giles Gilbert Scott, began in 1904 and the first of the famous Pier Head buildings, the Mersey Docks and Harbour Board Building, was begun in 1903. It would later be joined by the Royal Liver Building (1908–1911), and the Cunard Building (1914–1916), which made Liverpool one of the most advanced and most visually distinctive cities in the world.

6

A City at War

In the winter of 1906 Robert Cain fell ill with a respiratory complaint and for the first time in sixty years he was unable to attend to the business of the brewery. At first he stayed at 'Barn Hey', Hoylake, where he was surrounded by his children and grandchildren who lived nearby. When he showed signs of improvement he travelled to Llandrindod Wells to convalesce. But the wet spring became an even wetter summer and in June his condition deteriorated again. He returned to 'Barn Hey', where he died in the early hours of 19 July 1907, aged 82.

The next few days were a time of feverish activity. Apart from making arrangements for the funeral, Cain's sons moved quickly to keep the company running. At a board meeting on Tuesday 23 July, four days after the founder's death, the minutes recorded tributes to Robert Cain:

> Before proceeding to the business of the meeting the Board unanimously desired to place on record their deep sense of the irreparable loss the company had sustained by the death of the founder and principal shareholder of the company – Mr. Robert Cain – who died on the 19th July ... after a life devoted to the inception, the steady expansion, and the success of the undertaking.

The meeting itself must have been a sombre occasion, but there was also business to attend to, including the resignation of Charles Alexander Cain as secretary. He and his brother William Ernest would later lead the company together.

The local newspapers carried affectionate obituaries describing Cain as, among other things, 'a business man of great ability' (*Daily Post and Echo*), and celebrated his success. The burial took place in St James's Cemetery on Monday 22 July, in the shadow of the rock on which the building of Liverpool's Anglican Cathedral had just begun. This was the place where many of Liverpool's notable figures were buried, including William Brown (1784–1864), who paid for the William Brown Library; William Huskisson (1770–1830), killed in the world's first passenger train accident; Kitty Wilkinson (1786–1860), who turned her home into a public wash house during the cholera epidemics of the 1830s; and the painter William Daniels (1812–1880). Cain's father and mother are also buried there.

Cain died in what was then considered a heatwave. After months of rain, by mid-July Liverpool was enjoying sunny weather and the newspapers recorded temperatures of 68 °F (about 20 °C) in the shade on the day of his death. In fact the weather was so warm that many people took to diving and swimming in the docks, canals and rivers, resulting in a series of drownings and disappearances. The heatwave broke just after midnight on the day of Cain's funeral with a violent thunderstorm that caused flooding and more drownings across Liverpool, the North West and Wales.

The funeral itself was a grand affair. There was still thunder in the air as the cortege entered the cemetery and the mourners took their places among the graves. The chief mourners included Cain's surviving sons, Robert James, William and Charles, followed by Cain's grandsons. Among what the *Liverpool Courier* called the 'general body of mourners' were representatives of the Constitutional Association, the Licensed Victuallers Association, the Liverpool Brewers' Association, and many Aldermen, councillors and other dignitaries. Brewer Daniel Higson, whose firm would later take over the Mersey Brewery, and the painter George Hall Neale were also present.

Funerals of this size were an opportunity for members of Liverpool's ruling class to show their respects, but also to be seen to do so. On this occasion they had a large audience. Newspaper reports tell of a crowd of up to 3,000 people clamouring at the gates to be allowed into the cemetery. A large police presence made sure the official mourners were not disturbed, but Robert Cain's popularity among the people of Liverpool could be in no doubt. Such crowds underlined the future importance of his sons in the social and political life of the city. For his family, the funeral was of course much more than just a civic occasion or even an expression of public mourning. They were remembering a man whose dedication and hard work had given them a life of comfort, status and opportunity. While his self-belief and high expectations must have made him difficult to please, Robert Cain was remembered with great affection.

The funeral was also the moment at which the two sides of Cain's life came together in public. In life he seems to have kept a careful distance from his poorer relatives, leaving them to find their own way out of the slums from which he himself had escaped. But the link was not broken altogether. Besides the immediate family, two names stand out in the list of chief mourners. Here listed in the *Courier* are 'J. Reddy, sen. (nephew), and J. P. Reddy', names that link Robert Cain to his beginnings in Irish Liverpool and to his father. James Reddy Sr was the youngest son of Hannah and Pierce Reddy, Cain's sister and brother-in-law, who had looked after the brewer's father in the years leading up to his death in 1871.

It is unlikely that Robert Cain and his family had much to do with their Cain and Reddy relatives while he was alive. Stories passed down through the generations suggest a level of suspicion, perhaps at times even resentment. Cain, who is described in his obituaries as kindly but reserved, was not the kind of man to have been lavish with gifts. He had a strong belief in the character-building effects of hard work and like many self-made men he saw his own success as evidence that anyone could do the same if only they tried. He is reputed to have been overheard complaining when 'yet another family member' had been around the brewery looking for a job. Even so, he and his wife did not entirely neglect their less fortunate relatives and James Reddy was clearly a favourite. In the 1880s he was the licensee of a pub on Scotland Road, having no doubt been helped along by his uncle Robert. There is evidence also that another nephew, the son of Robert Cain's younger brother William, was helped to emigrate to Chile, where he and his wife stayed with relatives of Ann Cain and made a decent living.

Robert Cain's personal estate was settled on 25 October 1907 and valued at £411,017. That may not seem much by modern standards when small apartments in Liverpool's new docklands developments sell for £200,000 or more, but accounting for inflation this figure made Cain a very wealthy man indeed. At 2005 prices Cain's personal estate was worth over £28 million. It included the opulent mansion 'Barn Hey' on Meols Drive near Hoylake, horses and carriages, and a collection of paintings, including at least three by Daniels and one by Hall Neale. Over the previous decade Cain had gradually reallocated shares so that Charles and William Cain would be able to take over the company as easily as possible, and he had transferred a great deal of property to the company as a way of avoiding death duties. He also made generous provision in the form of shares in the company for his other surviving children, Robert James, Mary, Sarah, Lena and Gertrude, so that they would receive a substantial annual income.

For a family firm the death of the founder is always a powerful blow, but Charles and William faced more practical problems. Brewing in the Edwardian era was increasingly regulated and controlled by government. Magistrates had the power to remove licences where they thought there were too many in a particular area and Liverpool had always had more than its fair share of pubs and beer houses. Charles Cain was himself a city magistrate by then, but brewers were of course barred from making judgements on licensing issues. Despite these pressures Robert Cain and Sons was one of the most successful brewers in Britain and had continued to expand right up to Cain's death. In 1898 Cain's bought Wright's brewery on Church Road, Wavertree, and in 1906 negotiations began for the takeover of Joplin's, another well-known small Liverpool brewer.

In both cases Cain's acquired not only the breweries but their properties and pubs, including, in the case of Wright's, the famous Edge Hill Coffee House. As larger brewers continued to buy up licensed properties the market grew

fiercer and prices rose quickly. In the years before Cain's
death the firm had become well known for its property
deals and had expanded from the South End, its traditional
area of operation. In its obituary of the founder the *Daily
Post and Mercury* describes how Cain's made purchases
'in all parts of the city on an almost wholesale scale, and
in some instances fabulous sums have changed hands, as
much as £49,000 for a single house'. Besides buying houses
themselves, Cain's was famous for the quality of its refurbishments. Interestingly the *Daily Post and Mercury* does
not mention the Philharmonic or the Vines, but comments:
'Among the best-known houses belonging to the firm are
the Brook-House, Smithdown-road and another large establishment on Bryanston-road'.[54]

Although on the face of it Cain's had plenty of money
available for expansion, the cut-throat nature of the takeover
business is revealed on a Cain's brewery notecard on which
a hastily-scribbled contract was signed by the brewer Joplin.
In it he agreed not to do any deals on his licensed properties until after 16 October, which allowed the Cains time to
raise the cash and agree a deal on the pubs, which were then
worth £27,000. The takeover of Joplin's finally took place
early in 1907, and by then Robert Cain and Sons owned 200
pubs.

After the founder's death the brewery continued to thrive
despite a difficult market and tighter regulation, including
restricted opening times for pubs and rising rates of duty.
Apart from pressure on profits caused by the scramble to
buy properties in the years running up to the First World
War, and difficulties with suppliers, Cain's sons also had to

54 *Daily Post and Mercury*, 20 July 1907.

make decisions about their employees. As their business was increasingly carried out elsewhere this was not always easy. In August 1910, at an emergency board meeting held at the Savoy Hotel, London, William and Charles Cain and the solicitor W.W. Rutherford, who was by then an MP, considered the case of an employee named Moore, who had burst into the brewery carrying a gun and threatening to kill himself. Although nobody was hurt the board agreed that his conduct 'cannot be overlooked and that his connection with the company must terminate in his own interests as well as the interests of the company'. With a surprising degree of understanding and sympathy the board accepted Moore's resignation and offered him three months' pay.

Both William Ernest and Charles Alexander Cain were among the most influential and well-known brewers in Edwardian England. Less than seventy years had passed since their father had begun his brewing business in Limekiln Lane, yet by the beginning of the First World War his two remaining sons were establishment figures who could list many of the country's most powerful politicians among their friends and acquaintances. While their father had been content to do his politicking in the smoking rooms of Liverpool's gentlemen's clubs, his sons spread their influence further afield. By the 1920s, a century after their father had been born in poverty in County Cork and brought to live in the Liverpool slums, both William and Charles had been made baronets and owned large estates in the home counties.

The Edwardian years ended in May 1910 with the death of Edward VII. During his eight-year reign Liverpool had enjoyed a period of growth and development that would not be matched for another hundred years. The buildings around Dale Street and at the Pier Head made Liverpool one of the most architecturally advanced cities in Britain, and the completion of the Liver Building even gave it a 'skyscraper', just like its transatlantic cousin, New York. In 2004, in recognition of the city's remarkable architectural legacy, Liverpool's skyline was designated a World Heritage Site, which includes the Pier Head, the Albert Dock area, the Stanley Dock area, the commercial centre, the cultural quarter around William Brown Street, and the area of warehouses and merchants' houses around Duke Street.

The 700th anniversary of the city in 1907 had been a year for remembering the city's past and was celebrated with commemorative postcards, decorated trams, pageants and tableaux. During the summer the newspapers followed the celebration plans with pictures of banners and descriptions of great events in the city's history. The Edwardian era has since come to be remembered as an English golden age before the horrors of war and a century of violence. Cain's advertising from this period is typical of the imagery of the time: frothing pints of golden ale and huge wooden casks pulled on brightly coloured drays by well-groomed heavy horses. In the years that followed the ale would be weaker, the casks fewer, and the horses and brewery workers recruited to the battlefields of France.

But the realities of the Edwardian era were always some way removed from the idea of a golden age. Sectarian tensions and at times mob violence between Catholics and Protestants came to dominate Liverpool politics so that by the 1910 general election it had become a serious problem. Tony Lane reports Ramsay MacDonald's reputed statement that 'Liverpool is rotten and we had better recognise it'.[55] Industrial unrest was also starting to develop. Lane charts the growth of trade unionism from the 1890s and makes the point that by 1911, when Liverpool workers staged a successful strike, the local trade union movement had acquired a large membership. Unlike smaller towns and even many cities Liverpool's workforce was to a large extent casually employed and, until 1918, many did not have the vote:

> In pre-First World War Liverpool up to 60 percent of adult males in docklands were disenfranchised, and these were the very people who were flooding into the TGWU. Merchant seamen, for their part, could not register as absent voters and were therefore almost wholly excluded from the electorate.[56]

The low pay and casual employment that had been the experience of a great many Liverpudlians for a century or more created an atmosphere of antagonism between workers, their employers and their union leaders. Later in the century urban decay, industrial unrest and political division became so pervasive in Liverpool that they came to define the city in the eyes of outsiders and policymakers.

Also contrary to the comfortable image of Edwardian Britain was the issue of immigration. Liverpool's history of Irish immigration and the sectarianism that came with it had caused problems from the start, largely because of the huge numbers of people involved. In many ways the arrival of immigrants from Italy, China, the Caribbean and elsewhere went more smoothly, if only because they did not put so much pressure on the city's infrastructure. But that is not

55 Lane, *Gateway to Empire*, p. 137.
56 Lane, *Gateway to Empire*, p. 143.

to say that immigrants were always welcomed. In their essay 'Cosmopolitan Liverpool' Belchem and MacRaild make the point that although Liverpool prided itself on being a cosmopolitan city 'Non-Europeans in "cosmopolitan" Liverpool ... faced a more pernicious and pervasive mindset: racism'.[57]

Early twenty-first-century Liverpool is by and large a diverse and relatively peaceful city with a well-established Chinatown and significant populations of people who can trace their families back to India, Africa, the Caribbean, as well as Europe and elsewhere. But in the years running up to the First World War, Britain was gripped by the fear of being overrun by foreigners, and in Liverpool it was the Chinese who became the target of some of the most vicious attacks.

By the time the Aliens Act became law in 1906 Liverpool's Chinese community was established and settled. The Chinese ran laundries and other businesses and were generally considered among the most easy-going of communities. Many Chinese were seamen with no intention of staying, but those who had made their home in Liverpool were generally self-sufficient and made few demands on the city's resources. Robert Winder notes in *Bloody Foreigners* that after 1906 the Chinese were suspected of corrupting English women with opium and sex, though a 1907 report on the Liverpool Chinese noted that white women married to Chinese men were generally contented and well treated. Whatever the reality, the Chinese, who often arrived on ships with fewer than 20 passengers and thereby avoided the restrictions of the Aliens Act, became the 'yellow peril' and were caricatured as villains such as Dr Fu Manchu. But even as the Chinese were becoming the bogeymen of pre-war Britain, the mood was changing.

57 Belchem and MacRaild, 'Cosmopolitan Liverpool', p. 367.

As Winder explains: 'This general anti-foreign shiver soon found a new and specific target. As Britain lurched towards war in Europe, the position of Britain's German immigrants became first fragile, and then fraught.'[58]

By 1910 Liverpool had notable Greek, German, Italian, Russian, Polish and ethnic Jewish populations to go with its Irish, Welsh and Scottish inhabitants and the small black population which could trace its origins back to the port's role in the slave trade. As a major trading port it had always been the temporary home to seamen from all over the world and was generally a cosmopolitan place. But immigrant groups including Germans, Poles and Chinese all suffered attacks and persecution in the Edwardian period and after. In 1915, after the sinking of the Cunard liner *Lusitania* inflamed anti-German feelings, a full-scale riot broke out and raged for several days. Looting and arson destroyed 200 properties in Liverpool as well as across the Mersey in Birkenhead.

Liverpool's expansion and development continued as war began to seem more likely. In December 1912 the controversial reservoir scheme at Vrnwy, North Wales, made an additional 4.5 million gallons of fresh water available to the city, and in 1913 the Liverpool Exhibition was attended by King George V and Queen Mary, who also opened the Gladstone Dock at Seaforth, then the largest graving dock in the world and part of a massive docks complex built to accommodate the largest ships afloat. King George and Queen Mary returned to Liverpool in 1927 to open the completed Gladstone Dock system which boasted three miles of quays and 58 acres of open water. The first ship to use the dock in 1913 was

<hr/>

58 Robert Winder, *Bloody Foreigners: The Story of Immigration to Britain* (London: Abacus, 2005), p. 206.

Lusitania, later to become an emblem of German ruthlessness, but then simply one of the fastest transatlantic liners and an example of Liverpool's modernity.

By the start of the First World War, of Robert Cain's five sons only William and Charles were still alive. Robert James Cain, the eldest, had died aged 61 in 1909 and Herbert four years earlier aged 37 in 1905. William and Charles were educated at the Liverpool Institute and both made what were considered good marriages. Charles's wife came from a Nottinghamshire family that was socially well above the Cains but that had no male heirs. For this reason they combined their surnames to become Charles and Florence Nall-Cain. Their son, Ronald Nall-Cain, who was later the second Baron Brocket, became MP for Wavertree in 1930 at the age of 26.

When war broke out in July 1914 the Cain brothers were among the wealthiest and most influential men in Britain, with many properties in Liverpool, on the Wirral and in the home counties near London. Both William and Charles had become well-known for their generosity towards charities. In 1897 Charles helped found the Samaritan Hospital for Women in Upper Parliament Street, which later merged with the Hospital for Women. He and his wife helped fund new wards and equipment and he also sat on the board of the Royal Liverpool Infirmary, and was a governor of the Bluecoat Hospital and the Royal Southern Hospital. Charles also funded cancer research in the city. As war became more likely and Britain began to build its military strength, the Cain brothers offered the government two aircraft costing a total of £4,000, but the offer was not taken up. In the years that followed they would both make significant donations to the war effort.

From the start of the war Liverpool was a departure point for troops and a distribution centre for munitions. Passenger ships that had once crossed the Atlantic with migrants and visitors were converted for military service in the Gladstone Dock and elsewhere. While RMS *Lusitania* continued her ill-fated transatlantic passenger crossings despite the threat from enemy submarines, other liners, including Cunarders *Acquitania* and *Mauretania*, and White Star steamers *Britannic* and *Olympic*, were fitted out with deck guns and served as troop carriers and hospital ships. *Britannic* and *Olympic*, along with their sister ship *Titanic*, which sank in 1912, had been intended as the most luxurious ships in the world, but *Britannic*, the largest of the three, never saw service as a passenger liner. Arriving in Gladstone Dock fresh from the Harland and Wolff shipyards in Belfast she was requisitioned by the Admiralty and converted to a hospital ship before fitting out could even begin. The design of *Britannic* was modified to make her stronger even than the 'unsinkable' *Titanic*, but she hit a mine in the Aegean in 1916 and went down within an hour.

Besides its role as a wartime port Liverpool's hospitals became an important part of the war effort. Many of the large merchants' houses around Sefton Park and Hoylake were donated by wealthy families to serve as hospitals for wounded soldiers. William Cain, who by then spent much of his time at Wargrave Manor, Berkshire, donated his house 'Wilton Grange', West Kirby, to the nation in 1916 to be used as a home for 'totally and permanently disabled soldiers, to be called the Home of Honour'.[59] The offer was finally accepted in 1918 and the house, which overlooked the Royal

59 *The Times*, 6 March 1916.

Liverpool Golf Course and was near to his father's former home 'Barn Hey', became a convalescent home for injured officers. William Cain, who received a knighthood in 1917, supplemented his gift with a further £2,000 for fitting out. *The Times* went on to report that Sir William Cain and his wife Florence once donated a cheque for £20,000 to fund the Red Cross during the war.

The First World War brought thousands of troops through Liverpool. In the early years British and Irish soldiers left for Gallipoli from Liverpool and many of the largest regiments had depots and garrisons there. Siegfried Sassoon, who became famous as a war poet and an anti-war protestor, was stationed at the Royal Welch Fusiliers depot in Liverpool. Later, American and Canadian troops passed through the port on their way to the front.

Liverpool's role in the war was a significant one and Liverpudlians were closer to the hostilities than most people in Britain. Apart from the vast numbers of troops arriving and departing by sea and railway, the Mersey and the Irish Sea became a focus for hostile German activity. Submarines operated within a few miles of the mouth of the river and many ships were torpedoed or mined as they approached the port. While the sinking of *Lusitania* brought outrage and violence to the streets of the city, such frequent attacks so close to home seemed on the whole to strengthen the resolve of the city's inhabitants.

By the end of the war Liverpool, like much of Britain, was exhausted. In 1918 the city had to adjust to new political and economic conditions. For brewers the war years had not been kind and William and Charles Cain began to contemplate important changes in the brewery's future. The war had brought with it shortages in raw materials and much tighter licensing restrictions. In some areas, especially near to major munitions factories such as in Carlisle, breweries were nationalised. And while that did not happen in Liverpool, Prime Minister Lloyd George pointed to drink as a significant drag on the war effort. Beer was already weaker by 1914 than it had been in the mid-nineteenth century, but between 1914 and 1922 the strength of the average pint fell quite dramatically. This was partly as a result of government restrictions on the strength of beer itself and partly because of shortages of malt. Many brewers advertised the new weaker beer as 'Government Ale' to make it quite clear whose fault they thought it was.

At the beginning of the war Lloyd George had wanted to nationalise the whole brewing industry, but by 1920 the scheme had been dropped on the grounds of cost. The effect of the war was felt in terms of output as well as the strength of beer. Gourvish and Wilson state that in the case of Whitbread's Chiswell Street brewery in London, output fell by as much as 54 per cent; elsewhere 20 per cent or more was not unusual. In Dublin the strength of Guinness Extra Stout fell from 1074 degrees in 1916 to 1054 degrees in 1919, having dipped for a while as low as 1049 degrees in 1918, which was more or less the strength of the average pint of bitter at the time.[60] Yet although they complained about over-regulation and a more difficult market, brewers continued to increase their profits above inflation between 1913 and 1920.[61] Although the war years had been troublesome for brewers it was after the Armistice that the industry really began to suffer.

60 Gourvish and Wilson, *The British Brewing Industry*, p. 331.
61 Gourvish and Wilson, *The British Brewing Industry*, p. 335.

Several things came together to make life difficult for brewers in the post-war years. First, drinking beer had become quite expensive in comparison with other leisure activities and as people moved out of the crowded city slums they found themselves with more space and more ways to spend their off-duty hours. Secondly, through injury or death the war removed almost a million young men from the market, while brewers, with their expensive pubs and high overheads, found themselves competing with clubs serving cheap beer subsidised by member subscriptions. Finally, economic conditions took a turn for the worse after a brief economic boom in 1919. Put simply, there was less money to spend, and fewer people willing to spend it on beer.

Cain's was no exception. On 24 November 1920, not long after William Cain became a baronet, he and his brother arranged the purchase of Harding and Parrington, another Liverpool brewer. By then Robert Cain and Sons was one of Britain's six largest regional brewers, but the brewing industry was entering a period of great turmoil. Just as they had in the 1890s, brewing firms began to merge with one another to form ever larger organisations that dominated regional markets. In 1921 Charles Nall-Cain was also made a baronet and in September of that year the merger was announced of Cain's with Peter Walker, of Warrington and Burton, another top six regional brewer and a local rival of long standing.

The merger was an unequal one in terms of company size since the Warrington firm owned almost four times as many pubs and licensed properties as Cain's and had a 'book' value of over £7 million. Even so the prospectus, which was published in *The Times* on 3 October 1921, outlines the comparative profits of the two companies, and on those terms Cain's matched up well with its larger neighbour. For the five years leading up to 1921 Cain's profits averaged £359,815, while Walker's averaged £435, 210. Taking the combined profits of Cain's with the recently acquired Harding and Parrington, Robert Cain and Sons was within a few thousand pounds of Walker's.

Clearly these were huge sums of money for the time. Besides its impressive performance, much of the value of Cain's as a company lay in its properties, many of them purchased by Robert Cain during the nineteenth century. At the time of the merger Cain's properties were listed in the books at a value of over £1.8 million, but their true value must have been much higher. Noting that no new valuation had been done before the merger, the directors of Robert Cain and Sons gave an encouraging valuation of their own: 'These properties of which the greater portion was acquired last century could not, in the opinion of the Directors, be replaced today for twice that figure'.[62] The merged company had authorised capital of £5 million and owned over 1,000 pubs and other licensed properties.

On the face of it the larger company, Peter Walker and Son, was buying Robert Cain and Sons. But it was at the very least a marriage of equals, with the Cain brothers taking over as joint managing directors and Colonel J. Reid Walker as chairman; Sir William Cain's son, Ernest, was also elected to the board. In March the following year, at the first Annual General Meeting of the new company, *The Times* reported 'A Successful Amalgamation. Profits Well Maintained' and recorded the words of the chairman who saw 'encouraging

62 *The Times*, 3 October 1921.

prospects' in combining the two companies' industrial capacity.[63]

The name of the new company, Peter Walker (Warrington) and Robert Cain and Sons Ltd, did not have the ring of twenty-first-century company names but as an investment it was solid. Walker-Cain, as it was known for short, became over the next few decades one of the most powerful brewers in Britain. Over the course of the twentieth century it merged with many other companies, including Joshua Tetley, Ansell's and Ind Coope, and became part of Allied Breweries, later known as Carlsberg-Tetley, an international brewing corporation on a vast scale.

Robert Cain's brewery on Stanhope Street was built and extended throughout the second half of the nineteenth century and had served the Cain family business well. But by the 1920s, with brewers facing a sharp reduction in demand, many brewery buildings came up for sale. The Stanhope Street site was in need of modernisation and Walker's already owned breweries in Warrington and Burton. The company's profits suggest that these were performing well below their maximum efficiency and following the merger there were great savings to be made in combining the brewing operations. Within months of the merger, production of Cain's beers moved to Warrington. Showing a remarkable lack of sentimental attachment to their father's creation, in 1922 the Cain brothers put the Mersey Brewery up for sale and it was bought by Daniel Higson, a friend of Robert Cain's whose brewery also had a history dating back to the eighteenth century. Robert Cain's brewery would not produce beer with the Cain's name and tradition for another seventy years.

63 *The Times*, 31 March 1922.

7

The Higson's Years

The sale of the brewery building to Higson's in 1923 was a momentous event. The site had been bought sixty-five years earlier by Robert Cain and the brewery he built and developed was key to the success of his business. Daniel Higson himself had been present as a mourner at Robert Cain's funeral and, like Cain, was an influential figure in Liverpool's brewing community in the late nineteenth century. Unlike Robert Cain, however, Daniel Higson had inherited his brewery as a going concern. It had operated from premises on Cheapside since the 1790s but had existed under various names before then. By the time of the sale Higson's beer was brewed at the former Windsor Brewery on Upper Parliament Street.

The story of Higson's early years is described in some detail by Norman Cook in his book *Higson's Brewery, 1780–1980*, published to celebrate the company's bicentenary. The company had been founded by William Harvey, who began brewing around 1780 from premises on Dale Street. Harvey was also a builder and according to Cook seems to have brought his brother Enoch into the business to operate the new brewery at 60 Cheapside in the early 1790s. It was inherited by his nephew Robert Ellison Harvey in 1843. The business was taken over only a few years later by Thomas Howard, a wine and spirits merchant, and around 1850, just as Robert Cain was beginning his brewing business in Limekiln Lane, Howard recruited Daniel Higson as cashier and office manager.

Higson, born in Liverpool in 1830, was four years younger than Cain and came from a lower-middle-class family. He began working as a book-keeper and seemed to have no ambitions as an entrepreneur, working instead for Howard until 1865, when the brewer died. Cook explains:

> In 1865 Howard, a sick man, went off to Harrogate to take the waters at the spa. And there he died. Just before his death he revoked all former wills and prepared a new one.
>
> He left his entire personal estate and effects to his manager and cashier, Daniel Higson.[64]

Higson ran the business as Howard's executor until 1875 when it began operating under his own name. It became Daniel Higson Ltd in 1888. Like Cain's, the company fought the temperance movement, the gradual tightening of licensing hours, and the rising level of duty.

Although the company managed to grow throughout the late nineteenth century and up to the start of the war, Higson's did not expand as quickly as Robert Cain and Sons. Cain's firm hold on the board of his company meant that when times were hard it could adapt easily to new conditions. In contrast, the Higson's board was argumentative and divided. Cain remained a charismatic presence in the boardroom until the final few months of his life, while at the same time allowing his sons to develop their interest in the business and plan for the future. Daniel Higson, on the

64 Norman Cook, *Higson's Brewery, 1780–1980* (Liverpool: Kershaw Press Services, 1980), p. 16.

other hand, was a weak leader. Given a certain level of quality and attention to changing tastes, a medium-sized regional brewery in the second half of the nineteenth century was a business that could hardly fail. But as the market shrank and conditions became tougher, Robert Cain and others like him emerged as entrepreneurs in a different league.

To make matters worse, as he grew older Higson did not manage the transfer of power very well. The Higson's board, which included two of his sons, fought over the purchase of new brewery premises and in 1909 failed to make a deal with the Harvey family for the lease on the Cheapside Brewery. The brewery was sold from under them in 1912 and Higson's finally settled on the Windsor Brewery on Upper Parliament Street. The Windsor Brewery was then owned by the family of William Blackburn, Robert Cain's former brewer, and it was apparently sold to settle gambling debts. Higson's renamed it the Cheapside Brewery and brewing began there on 31 January 1914. Seven months later, on 31 August, Daniel Higson died at his home in Blundellsands.

While Cain's came through the war years in good shape and was able to merge with Walker's on comparable, if not equal, terms, Norman Cook describes Higson's as a company in turmoil:

> The war years brought problems for most brewery companies but in general they survived them well enough. Higson's, however, had problems which were not solely the product of wartime difficulties. Boardroom differences and financial problems which had their origins in the pre-war period were weighing heavily on the company's operations and, perhaps inevitably, the decision had to be taken to sell the business as a going concern.[65]

65 Cook, *Higson's Brewery*, p. 21.

There was interest from several local brewers, but in the end Higson's was sold in 1918 to J. Sykes and Co. for £118,500 in a deal masterminded and managed by solicitor William Corlett, a partner in the firm of Bremner and Sons.

W. E. Corlett was a brilliant company lawyer who believed in the virtues of hard work and dedication to business. Within a matter of weeks he had been appointed first managing director of the new firm, and soon afterwards he became chairman. At a time when many breweries were facing mergers and closures, Corlett turned Higson's around. By 1920 the company was looking for ways to expand and when the Walker-Cain merger took place Corlett saw an opportunity to move into one of the largest breweries in Liverpool. Negotiations to buy the Stanhope Street brewery began in 1922 and were completed in 1923. The brewery was sold to Higson's for £100,000 and Corlett set about making it his own.

Corlett was like Robert Cain in many ways. He had a strong work ethic and a good eye for business opportunities. Like Cain he was renowned for keeping regular and long working hours and was a dynamic and charismatic leader. He was also keenly aware of the value of advertising. In the nineteenth century brewers such as Robert Cain had used billboards, signs in pub windows, signwriting on brewery drays and other similar methods to advertise their ales. Advertising informed rather than entertained. Cain's 'Superior Ales and Stouts' was a phrase well known in Liverpool in 1900. But as competition intensified in the lean years of the 1920s, advertisers became more playful and more inventive. Corlett lost no time in marketing Higson's as a modern, dynamic brewer with a firm Liverpool tradition.

The centrepiece of Corlett's plan for Higson's was the Stanhope Street brewery. Under Robert Cain it had been known as the Mersey Brewery and its imposing terracotta walls were decorated with the initials 'RC' and other Robert Cain and Sons symbols. Soon after taking over the brewery, Corlett removed much of the Robert Cain branding and replaced it with 'Daniel Higson Brewery Established 1850'. Since the brewery is now a listed building the Higson's name will be forever etched in the walls of Robert Cain's creation, but traces of Cain's ownership remain in the twenty-first century, including the gazelle motif above the entrance to the yard and on the corner of the building above the Brewery Tap. Since it has no real significance in the history of Higson's as a company it is likely that the date 'Established 1850' also carries over from the Robert Cain era.

Beyond the brewery, Higson's advertising played on popular interests and ideas. Cook explains that one advertisement from 1925 'proclaimed: "Something to look forward to ... Higson's Genuine Ales". Within this there appeared an artist's impression of the Mersey Tunnel, not due to be opened for a further nine years.'[66] Another forward-looking campaign in 1926 involved a competition to come up with a new slogan which drew 300,000 entries from around the country and resulted in the slogan 'It's Noted, it's Quoted, it's Voted The Best'. The competition was apparently won by an unemployed boilermaker who declared that he would deposit most of the money in the bank. The reality was different: 'it was said that he had spent £90 out of his £100 [prize money] in three weeks'.[67] At around the same

66 Cook, *Higson's Brewery*, p. 23.
67 Cook, *Higson's Brewery*, p. 27.

time Higson's anticipated the well-known national 'Beer is Best' campaign of 1933 with the slogan 'Higson's: The Best for You', and followed it up with the line 'Brewed in the Finest Brewery in the British Isles'. Other firms took a similar approach at the time, including Guinness, whose 'My Goodness, My Guinness' campaign was created by no less a figure than crime writer Dorothy L. Sayers, famous for her detective novels featuring Lord Peter Wimsey.

Corlett's innovative approach to advertising and marketing helped keep the company going at a time of rising unemployment and looming economic trouble. Higson's managed to fend off competition from much larger rivals, including Walker-Cain, and increased its holdings of public houses. The transition from horse-drawn drays to motor wagons helped the company supply increasing numbers of pubs on both sides of the Mersey as well as Sykes outlets in Yorkshire and the North East. Corlett bought smaller companies, including Joseph Jones of Knotty Ash and Spraggs, a small brewery in Wallasey, and supplied their pubs from Stanhope Street.

Liverpool in the 1920s was a relatively prosperous place. While the effects of the First World War could still be felt and labour disputes, including the 1926 General Strike, reflected low pay and difficult times, the port kept Liverpool in business. The city's suburbs grew quickly as slum clearance and large-scale construction of corporation housing raised living standards, while cinemas, theatres and sport had become the major leisure activities. Cinema in particular seems to have exploded in Liverpool during the 1920s. Colin Pooley outlines its growth:

It is estimated that in 1931 there were on average some 576,000 cinema attendances in Liverpool each week, representing around two-thirds of the population. In fact many people attended more than once a week and it was suggested that about 40 per cent of the population attended the cinema regularly with 25 per cent of this number going at least twice a week. Of the films shown in Liverpool, social dramas, thrillers and comedies dominated.[68]

As in most large cities, cinemas were springing up everywhere, in Liverpool more than doubling in number to 69 by 1931.

Liverpool was also acquiring a reputation as a sporting city. Fifty years earlier it had been notorious for bare knuckle boxing and dog fights, but by the 1920s nearby Southport had become a centre for motor racing while horse racing and greyhound racing were also popular. With the help of the cinema newsreels the Grand National, held at Aintree since the 1830s, was a national spectacle.

But it is football that has dominated the Liverpool sporting scene in the twentieth century. Everton FC won their first League Championship in 1890–91 and the FA Cup in 1905–06, but the late 1920s and early 1930s saw the club win many honours. Playing in front of regular crowds of 30,000 or more, striker Dixie Dean scored 60 goals in 39 league games in the 1927–28 season, when Everton won their third league title. By 1939 the club held five league titles and had won the FA Cup twice. Local rivals Liverpool FC also blossomed in the 1920s, winning back-to-back league titles in 1922 and 1923. By the beginning of the Second World War they had won four league titles.

68 Colin G. Pooley, 'Living in Liverpool: The Modern City', in Belchem (ed.), *Liverpool 800*, p. 239.

Despite periods in which they underperformed, the city's two football clubs have been among the most successful British clubs of the past one hundred years. In the 1970s and 1980s Liverpool dominated the domestic league and cup competitions, but Everton remained their biggest rivals, taking the league title in 1984–85 and 1986–87 to keep the honour in the city throughout the 1980s. Leaving aside both clubs' success in cup competitions at home and in Europe, a measure of the city's importance in the world of football is the fact that a Liverpool club topped the English league in 18 of the 30 seasons between 1961 and 1990.

Liverpool was emerging as a footballing powerhouse in the 1920s, but in other ways too it was developing into an important twentieth-century city. The unfinished Anglican cathedral was consecrated in 1924 while new housing schemes spread out to Dingle, Allerton, Knotty Ash and Knowsley. Slum clearances gradually moved people into suburban estates, mostly built by the corporation. The Queensway Tunnel under the Mersey, which was first broken through in 1927, was officially opened by King George V on 18 July 1934 in a ceremony watched by a crowd of 200,000 people. This further expanded the city's commuter belt, which by then was also reaching Crosby and Maghull to the north. By 1929 Liverpool's prosperous centre thronged with trams, buses and cars, the Mersey was busy with ships and, as the success of Frank Hornby's Meccano factory demonstrated, manufacturing was thriving. City planners even began developing innovative new roads. The dual carriageway County Road to Southport, opened in 1938, was one of the earliest roads of its type in the country.

Liverpool's credentials as a modern city were not in

doubt, but in some ways it remained a troubled place. The issue of immigration was an ongoing problem for some Liverpudlians who supported tight restrictions on the rights of immigrants. In the 1920s, for example, Indian immigrants were not allowed to carry full passports and were likely to be stopped and searched at any time. In 1927 Liverpool's Indian population staged a protest against their treatment in the city. Robert Winder highlights the point of tension: 'It was becoming awkward enough to insist that India was British without having to explain that Indians were also "aliens"'.[69] For Liverpool this was familiar territory. While immigrants from the Irish to the Chinese were tolerated as long as they looked after themselves, when they seemed to be taking advantage things were different. By 1938 over a quarter of seamen in the British merchant fleet were Indian and seemed to pose a direct threat to the livelihoods of Liverpool families.

The situation was not helped by rising unemployment after 1930. The 1929 Wall Street crash signalled the beginning of the Great Depression in the United States and started a global downturn. Unemployment in Britain doubled to around 20 per cent of the workforce within a matter of months and most of the damage was done in Northern cities, including Liverpool. By the time of the Jarrow protest march in 1936 conditions for many working-class families, especially in the North of England, had returned to Victorian standards of poverty and squalor.

In contrast, the inter-war years saw William and Charles Cain rise to the highest levels of wealth and social position. When Sir William Cain, first Baronet Cain, died at his

69 Winder, *Bloody Foreigners*, p. 286.

estate, Wargrave Manor, on 5 May 1924, he was chairman of Walker-Cain, a governor of Liverpool University, and one of Britain's most powerful business leaders. His younger brother Charles became a baronet in 1921 and was raised to the peerage in 1933, taking his title of Lord Brocket from his country seat, Brocket Hall, in Hertfordshire. The issue of how Charles came to be given his hereditary peerage is not now important. Both he and his brother were significant contributors to charity and besides his business positions Charles served as High Sheriff of Hertfordshire and as chairman of the Welwyn Petty Sessions. They were both important men who alongside their own success had contributed a great deal to Britain's public life. But this seems to have been the time in which the story of Robert Cain's Irish ancestry became clouded, perhaps because the newly created peer wanted to assert an aristocratic lineage.

Charles, who died on 21 November 1934, traced his family back to the O'Cahans, described in his *Times* obituary as 'a family of great antiquity and importance in Northern Ireland. They adopted the wild cat as their device, which the late peer took for his crest and as supporters of his coat of arms.'[70] *Burke's Peerage* changed its entry on the Cain family in the 1930s. Early editions list Robert Cain's father as James Cain of Dublin, who married Mary Dean in 1824. Later editions give his birthplace as Galway, his marriage to Mary Deane of Cork in 1824, and his social background as belonging to the gentry. Neither version of the story appears to be true.

From the point of view of the Higson's board the 1930s was a difficult decade. On the one hand, the economic

70 *The Times*, 22 November 1934.

troubles meant people had less money to spend on luxuries like beer. But on the other, the growth of large suburban housing estates opened up new opportunities. Large, well-furnished pubs were built to serve the inhabitants of the new estates, and brewers such as Higson's were able to trade licensed premises in the old slum areas for new ones in the suburbs. Bottled beer also became more popular in the 1920s and 1930s, largely as a result of improvements in housing which meant more people wanted to spend their leisure time at home. Higson's bottled brands such as Double Top and Stingo – a barley wine – were among the most popular in Liverpool.

Despite increasing sales of bottled beer, overall sales of beer fell in the years leading up to the Second World War, by as much as 33 per cent according to some measures. Gourvish and Wilson note that government estimates of the fall in brewing industry profits went from '£26 million in 1930 to £23 million in 1932 and only £16 million in 1933, over a third lower than in 1930'.[71] Many brewers continued to turn in comfortable and easy profits even as the industry contracted, but Higson's struggled at times. Norman Cook points out that the company was given 18 months' credit by its maltster, Paul's, to see it through a rough patch in 1932. Between 1921 and 1940 the number of brewing companies in Britain halved from roughly 900 to around 400. But Higson's, operating out of Robert Cain's famous brewery, managed to survive and on 12 January 1937 it was incorporated as Higson's Brewery Ltd, a new company with £1 million of authorised capital. J. Sykes and Co. Ltd, the former parent company, became a subsidiary. By the end of the 1930s economic conditions

71 Gourvish and Wilson, *The British Brewing Industry*, p. 342.

were improving and Higson's was again in profit to the tune of £100,133 in 1938.

After the troubles of the 1930s the war years posed an even greater problem for the Liverpool brewer. As war loomed it was clear to most people in Liverpool that the city was key to the country's survival and would be a prime target for German bombs. The tonnage of goods coming and going through the port of Liverpool each year had risen from just over 19 million tonnes in 1914 to almost 21 million in 1939, and while the rapid expansion of the late Victorian era was over, the port of Liverpool remained one of Britain's most important assets. As Brian Perrett points out in his book *Liverpool: A City at War*, at the beginning of the Second World War Liverpool was still a good place for manufacturing and trade.

Perrett explains that preparations for war began as early as 1937 when the first volunteers were recruited to the emergency services. There was also a determination not to repeat mistakes made during the First World War, when many essential dock workers were accepted for duty on the front line. Liverpudlians realised they would have to defend their city and volunteered in large numbers to be special constables, volunteer fire fighters and Air Raid Precautions (ARP) wardens. Perrett notes that by September 1939 the Liverpool ARP employed 2,500 full-time wardens and over 15,000 volunteers. As they had many times before, the people of Liverpool prepared to face hardship with determination and pride.

It would be almost a year before Liverpool saw its first enemy action, when reconnaissance planes dropped small numbers of bombs around Merseyside in June 1940. Attacks did not begin in earnest until September that year when German bombers visited Liverpool roughly every other night, hitting Walton prison and warehouses throughout the docks complex. Bombing continued through to December, killing many hundreds of people and destroying homes, buildings and shipping. The Irish Sea was mined and enemy submarines again patrolled the area around the mouth of the Mersey, attacking shipping and emphasising the extent to which the country depended on Liverpool for food, munitions and other supplies. But compared with what was to come these attacks were light.

As in the First World War, food restrictions were put in place and for brewers there were severe limits on the amount of barley and other ingredients that could be used for beer. New licensing restrictions closed pubs at 9 o'clock each night as a precaution, but by then the pubs were mostly empty as people stayed at home or took to the shelters. Unlike the First World War, however, when enemy action was limited to the estuary and Irish Sea, the bombing raids had a direct effect on Higson's brewery. The Coburg Dock, situated at the bottom of Stanhope Street within sight of the brewery, had for half a century or more been an important grain importing dock. The whole area came under bombardment in the autumn and winter of 1940. Perrett explains that the aircraft of Luftflotte 3 delivered their first effective attack on Liverpool on the night of 26 September:

> Widespread damage was caused in the area of Wapping, King's, Queen's, Coburg and Brunswick Docks, destroying thirteen warehouses and the Admiralty stores at Canning Place. The Dock Board and Cunard offices were hit ...[72]

72 Brian Perrett, *Liverpool: A City at War* (Burscough: Hugo Press, 1990), p. 82.

The brewery stood no more than a few hundred metres from the centre of this attack and while it is not known whether it was hit on this occasion, Robert Cain's 1887 extension to the 1838 Hindley brewhouse was destroyed by bombing at about this time.

Despite the damage and the loss of life in these early raids Liverpool did not come under sustained attack until 1941. The port continued to function and while many ships were damaged and sunk as they unloaded their cargoes, they were quickly repaired or removed. A combination of Liverpool grit, community spirit and a feeling that the tables would soon be turned kept the city going in those years. The catastrophic 'Liverpool Blitz' did not take place until May 1941, but when it came it was ferocious.

For anyone who did not live through it, the extent of the destruction of Liverpool in the spring and early summer of 1941 is hard to imagine. The Victorian city, where the merchant princes had made their fortunes and where Robert Cain had built his brewing empire, was bombed almost out of existence. In the first few days of May, culminating in a massive bombing raid on the 3rd and 4th, Liverpool burned. Perrett describes the scene: 'Almost all the buildings within the area embraced by Lord Street, Paradise Street, Canning Place and South Castle Street were either destroyed outright or so severely damaged as to warrant instant demolition'.[73] Some of the most striking images of Liverpool from this period show Lewis's famous department store gutted, houses collapsed and whole tracts of the city reduced to rubble. The great Victorian cultural quarter, the city's confident answer to 'Albertopolis' in the mid-nineteenth century, also

73 Perrett, *Liverpool: A City at War*, p. 98.

suffered severe damage. The museum took a direct hit, the library was destroyed by fire, and the Walker Art Gallery was also damaged. The famous Custom House, built in 1826, was completely destroyed. Broken water mains made fighting the fires even harder and many buildings burned simply because nobody could do anything to prevent the fire spreading.

The intensive bombing lasted through May and into June 1941, killing over 1,700 people and leaving 1,200 seriously injured. Such were the numbers that the dead were buried in mass graves, including 550 in a vault at Anfield cemetery. This was the most serious bombing suffered by Liverpool during the war and it left large areas of the city destroyed, over 50,000 people homeless, and the docks, Liverpool's greatest asset, in ruins. Shattered water mains and severed electricity and telephone cables made the task of clearing the rubble even harder, while broken gas mains were a serious hazard. It was August before Liverpool's roads and railways were working properly again. Over 40 wrecks littered the dock system, posing a threat not only to shipping but to the entire British war effort.

Perrett describes the extent of Liverpool's collapse in terms of shipping and tonnages. In the week ending 26 April, he says, 181,562 tons of cargo landed in Liverpool: 'By 3 May, after the attack had been in progress two days, it had fallen to 145,596 tons. On 10 May the full effects of the attack were revealed by a weekly landing total reduced to only 35,026 tons.'[74] But Liverpool was to recover quickly. The comeback city began to dust itself off even while the attacks continued. By the end of May weekly landings were back up to 93,000 tons and by mid-June the docks were almost

74 Perrett, *Liverpool: A City at War*, p. 126.

back to normal: 'during the week ended 14 June no less than 126,936 tons were landed'.[75]

The Second World War marked a turning point in the history of Liverpool in a way that it did not for many other British cities. The extent of the destruction meant that most of the city centre had to be rebuilt or redeveloped, but at a more human level the city was also transformed. The last of the courts were swept away in one of the most ambitious slum clearance programmes in British history, while manufacturing, rather than shipping, became Liverpool's main source of income.

But perhaps the most significant change was in how Liverpool and Liverpudlians were seen by the outside world and how they saw themselves. Liverpool had sustained similar damage to the capital during the 1941 bombing, but it was not reported because Liverpool's strategic value was far too significant. Had news of the destruction become widely known not only would it have been a boost to German morale, but it would have dealt a severe blow to confidence at home. London's plucky cockney became the iconic figure of the homefront in wartime Britain while Liverpool suffered in silence. In Liverpool itself, however, the lack of attention to the city's problems did not go unnoticed. What effect this may have had on the character of the city in the second half of the twentieth century is a matter for speculation, but it can only have hardened the sense of Liverpool's separateness from the mainstream of British life.

During the post-war years Liverpool traded on the cultural stock exchange as a city of comedy, poetry, music and avant-garde art. To the rest of the country it remained a

75 Perrett, *Liverpool: A City at War*, p. 126.

tough, hard-working, gritty Northern city, and its musicians, artists and performers lived up to that reputation with humour, sharp wit and hard-headed ambition. Yet by the 1970s, when Britain experienced one of the most severe economic downturns in its history, Liverpool was a city that seemed to have lost its purpose. In the eyes of the world Liverpool's famous resilience had turned to self-pity. Crime, poverty and social collapse had replaced trade, industry and innovation as the city's contributions to British life.

8

Boom and Bust

At the end of the war, as flags and bunting fluttered over the bomb sites, Liverpool celebrated with a victory parade and reflected on the challenges it had faced and overcome. What lay ahead was a challenge of a different kind. In the immediate post-war years Liverpool was an optimistic and forward-looking place with a booming economy and a promising future. The recovery from wartime destruction was swift and impressive. Within two decades Liverpool was reinventing itself once again as a modern, dynamic and stylish city. And yet somehow the city lost its way. The second half of the twentieth century would see Liverpool's position as a maritime powerhouse gradually erode and its industries struggle. By 1981, when the Toxteth riots destroyed 500 buildings and damaged many more, the city Robert Cain had bossed a century earlier was an emblem of political failure and collapse.

The 1936 Liverpool Corporation Act had granted the city permission to build and own property on a scale that was unknown in British urban history. After 1945 Liverpool took full advantage, setting about solving its housing crisis with energy and imagination. Prefabricated housing

took care of the immediate problem but during the 1950s
and 1960s almost 200,000 Liverpudlians found new homes in
the municipal housing estates as far away as Speke, Huyton,
Croxteth and Netherley. Jon Murden describes the growth
of Kirkby, one of the largest of the new townships: 'The first
municipal house was built in Kirkby in 1952, before which
about 3,000 people lived in a predominantly rural area. By
1961, 10,000 dwellings had been constructed and by 1965 the
population was 52,000.'[76]

Liverpool's housing problems dated back 150 years to
the early nineteenth century. In 1954 some 33,000 dwellings
in areas such as Toxteth and Everton were judged unfit for
human habitation and by then many had been slums for a
century or more. In Toxteth, notorious in the 1880s for its
infant mortality rate and deaths from 'fever', even as late as
the 1980s damp, cold, unhealthy houses were not uncommon.
In many cases slum dwellings in the 1950s suffered problems
with sewerage that would have been familiar to Robert Cain
while he was growing up on Bent Street in the 1830s. It was
eventually decided that around one third of the city's housing
stock would have to be replaced, a plan that would take over
three decades to complete. In place of the rows of Victorian
terraces rose modernistic tower blocks, while further out
neat estates of semi-detached houses spread across fields.

But although the need for new housing was beyond
dispute, the scale of the project failed to take account of
the depth of the roots that had to be pulled up. Despite the
optimism and the good intentions, the relocation of old
communities left inner-city neighbourhoods empty and
disfigured. Roger McGough, who worked as a teacher at St

76 Murden, 'City of Change and Challenge', p. 396.

Kevin's Comprehensive School for Boys in Kirkby, describes what the new estates were like in the late 1950s:

> In the fifties, when the old back-to-backs along Scotland Road and south to the Dingle were pulled down, families who had lived in the city for generations were offered the opportunity to relocate to the countryside. It may have sounded appealing, the intentions may even have been the best, but it was a disaster ... When I arrived [in September 1959] to take up my post, there were a few mobile shops and a church, but no pubs, clubs, shopping centres, cafés, sports centres, or any ingredients vital to nourishing a community.[77]

This fragmentation of the city's old communities played a part in Liverpool's collapse in the 1970s and 1980s, but in the short term the pace of relentless building and rebuilding kept the city moving.

In the city centre bomb sites lingered for longer than most people wanted, but by the early 1960s work was well under way to redevelop the whole central area. Clayton Square and St John's Precinct were part of an ambitious plan to pedestrianise the central shopping streets, while traffic was routed away from the city through a second Mersey road tunnel. The 'old-fashioned' transport networks, such as the Overhead Railway and the trams, were shut down and dismantled in 1956 and 1957. A modern transport system in the 1950s was essentially a system built around the car. Between 1955 and 1962 Aintree hosted the British motor racing grand prix five times and when Ford opened its Halewood car manufacturing plant in 1963 Liverpool had become in many ways a motor city.

The process of demolition and redevelopment was only one of the challenges faced by the board of Higson's

---

77 McGough, *Said and Done*, p. 108.

brewery in the 1950s. The bombs had destroyed many pubs and damaged part of the brewery, while wartime licensing restrictions, the early closing time, as well as reduced supplies of raw materials had all affected the business. Slum clearance included the demolition of many pubs in the post-war period and meant customers had to be won again in their new suburban neighbourhoods. To add to the problems faced by Higson's, several members of the board were nearing retirement, leaving the company with uncertain leadership at a time when decisive action had to be taken.

William Ernest Corlett remained at the helm of Higson's, but he had recruited his grandson Gerald in 1947, and by 1955 the 30-year-old had joined the board as its youngest member by far. His grandfather, who held the post of chairman until his death in 1960 at the age of 93, remained an active leader, but Gerald, known as Gerry, was free to introduce new ideas and new technologies. Following in the tradition set by Robert Cain, Higson's began a programme of modernisation and improvement that lasted into the 1980s. An article about Higson's in the *Illustrated Liverpool News* in September 1965 carries an echo of Cain's own words from eighty years before: 'In any business one must continually keep an eye open for future developments'.

Throughout the 1950s, as Liverpool enjoyed economic good times, Higson's expanded. Fuel rationing brought a temporary reprieve for the horse-drawn brewery dray in the 1940s, but for long-distance transport modern trucks were essential. In 1955 Higson's took control of J. Addy and Co. Ltd, the haulage contractor that had carried Higson's ales around the region for many years. The fleet of Addy's trucks kept expanding as demand for Higson's ales grew, and by 1976 a large transport garage was built on Beaufort and Brassey Streets, fifty metres or so from the main brewery building. Next door was a cask distribution shed, while across the road, just behind the old brewery stable, was the bottling store. In 1962 Higson's bought property on the corner of Dale Street and North Street in the city centre to serve as the company headquarters, office space and a wine and spirit warehouse. By 1965 Higson's had control of 174 pubs and employed 1,300 people, most of them on Merseyside.

Like breweries across the country Higson's spent a great deal of money on improving its pubs. Nationally over £13 million was spent by brewers on public house refurbishment in 1954–1955 alone. According to Norman Cook, between 1955 and 1980, the company's bicentennial year, Higson's bought seven pubs, rebuilt five old ones and built a further 27 brand new pubs on new estates and other sites in the city.[78] Although the total number of pubs controlled by the company declined very slightly in the same period, Higson's was one of the few breweries in the region to increase its stock of pubs as a proportion of the total in the area. This success is reflected in the profits, which rose steadily throughout the 1960s and 1970s.

Part of the reason for Higson's success was its status as a distinctively Liverpool brand. Working for Higson's was a matter of pride and former employees of the brewery remember their time there with great fondness. The Corlett family, who managed and ran the brewery for almost sixty years, are also remembered as strong, assertive, but benevolent leaders. Gerry Corlett, who took over as joint managing director alongside Claude Price in 1964, and who took sole

78 Cook, *Higson's Brewery*, p. 38.

charge in 1967 when Price died, managed the company's expansion and development through some of Liverpool's most exciting and turbulent years. But as the world of business began to change in the 1970s industrial disputes gradually soured the traditional relationship of loyalty and care that existed between brewers and their workers.

When Corlett joined the board in 1955 Liverpool was known in the country at large as a city of faded glory, of bomb-scarred streets, a port in decline, of gaudy working-class tastes, and wry humour. In Liverpool, as in the rest of the country, unemployment was low, wages were relatively high and opportunities were everywhere. Wartime troop convoys and the 'Cunard Yanks', Liverpool men working the passenger liners across the Atlantic, brought American music, tastes and fashions and gave the city a transatlantic flavour. Liverpool's burgeoning art and music scene is an indication of the confidence of the times. While the city was hardly unique in having clubs, pubs and theatres that put on live bands, comedy shows and off-beat dramas, there does seem to have been something about Liverpool that encouraged them to be bold.

Perhaps it was the old Atlantic-facing attitude, perhaps it was a sense that anything was possible in a city that was being rebuilt from the ground up, perhaps it was the city's tradition of burlesque and circus. But whatever it was, in the 1960s Liverpool's contribution to the cultural life of Britain went far beyond what might have been expected. When John Lennon and Paul McCartney began performing as the Quarrymen in October 1957 they were just two normal teenagers with an enthusiasm for American music. Later, as members of the Beatles, they became a Liverpool export at least as influential on world culture as Liverpool's merchant princes had been in the 1880s. The Beatles are of course the most famous of Liverpool's cultural exports of that time, but they were far from alone. Their early style was part of what became known as 'Merseybeat', which emerged as a local interpretation of skiffle, and was developed by Liverpool bands such as the Searchers, Gerry and the Pacemakers, Rory Storm and the Hurricanes, and the Swinging Blue Jeans. Liverpool even had its own weekly music paper, *Mersey Beat*.

In other arts too Liverpool made its mark. 'Liverpool 8', the city's bohemian quarter, took in what became the Everyman Theatre, the Philharmonic Hall and the surrounding streets. Adrian Henri described it in a poem:

Rodney St pavement stretching to infinity
Italian garden by the priest's house
seen through the barred doorway on Catherine St
pavingstones worn smooth by summer feet
...
Gambier Terrace loud Beatle guitars from the first floor
Sam painting beckoning phantoms hiding behind painted
words bright colours[79]

This was the part of Liverpool where young intellectuals mingled with ambitious pop performers, including Lennon and McCartney, classical musicians, college and university lecturers, artists and hangers-on. Bob Dylan, at the height of his notoriety as the singer who brought electric guitars to folk music, performed in Liverpool during his British tour in 1965 and in the same year American Beat poet Allen Ginsberg visited the city and proclaimed it 'the center of consciousness of the universe'.

79 From 'Poem for Liverpool 8' by Adrian Henri.

In 1967 Henri, along with Roger McGough and Brian Patten, published an anthology of poetry called *The Mersey Sound*, which appeared as Book 10 of the Penguin Modern Poets series. The book did much to revive poetry in the 1960s and 1970s and became one of the best-selling poetry anthologies of all time. Part of the book's appeal was its wit and frankness about urban life, but the poems also carried with them a distinctively Liverpool style that was highly fashionable at the time. McGough recalls performing at Streate's Coffee Bar on Mount Pleasant which 'was to poetry what the Cavern was to rock 'n' roll' and remembers '"Tonk", faux anarchist whose Beat rantings seemed to have come straight out of Greenwich Village'.[80]

The wry style of the Liverpool art scene fused poetry with pop art, comedy and music, and became central to a British version of the Beat revolution that was taking place in the United States. Scouse voices were frequently heard on highbrow radio and television arts shows in the 1960s. The Liverpool accent contrasted sharply with the old-fashioned establishment vowels of the BBC's interviewers and seemed subversive, offbeat and terribly modern. Humour was an important part of the Liverpool counter-culture as it was for Liverpudlians in general. In the world of popular entertainment comedians such as Arthur Askey and Tommy Handley had reinforced the city's existing reputation for making jokes in the face of adversity after the war. The popularity of their successors, including Ken Dodd and Jimmy Tarbuck, gave the impression that British TV in the mid-1960s was being taken over by cheeky Scousers.

---

80 McGough, *Said and Done*, p. 129.

The more established arts also flourished in Liverpool in the 1960s. This was a time during which the Royal Liverpool Philharmonic Orchestra, based at the Philharmonic Hall, was considered one of the best symphony orchestras in the world. From 1957 the Walker Art Gallery hosted the biennial John Moores Exhibition and was significant in the early career of artist David Hockney. Liverpool's theatres faced tough competition from television, but several managed to survive, attracting stars such as Frank Sinatra and directors such as Sam Wanamaker. Liverpool's curious blend of mainstream entertainment, the traditional arts and ground-breaking avant-garde creativeness was unique. It is captured on the Beatles' most celebrated and dramatic album, *Sergeant Pepper's Lonely Hearts Club Band*, in sounds from the dance-hall, the circus and the fairground, orchestral strings, and songs about suburban life. But as Jon Murden comments, 'Ironically at the point when the Beatles had reached their creative zenith the Liverpool music scene was in the process of burning out'.[81]

By the mid-1960s Liverpool was at the height of a golden age that almost matched the peak of 1910. The building of the controversial Roman Catholic Cathedral, now acknowledged as one of the great British buildings of the twentieth century but reviled in 1967 as a monstrosity, was a sign of the optimism, energy and bravery of the city's leaders. But as the pace of housing development and regeneration slowed, cracks were beginning to show in Liverpool's post-war prosperity. The docks had been struggling since the decline of the transatlantic passenger lines and factories were closing at an alarming rate. People began to move away from the city

81 Murden, 'City of Change and Challenge', p. 425.

and over the next forty years the population would fall by almost half from its 1960 peak of 700,000.

By 1971 diners in the French restaurant at the top of the newly opened 450-foot high St John's Beacon looked down from their revolving perch on a city that was shedding jobs to regional rivals such as Manchester and Birmingham, but also abroad. Vast tracts of Liverpool had been levelled by slum clearance and regeneration projects, while increasing numbers of manufacturing businesses were shutting down altogether. In the case of the port, Liverpool's geography was against it when it came to competing with European-facing ports such as Dover and Folkestone. And while the actual tonnage passing though the port at the end of the century was higher than in 1960, the container traffic required a much smaller workforce. From confident full employment in 1965, the year of Liverpool FC's famous FA Cup victory under Bill Shankly, by 1979 the city was struggling with an unemployment rate of over 12 per cent.

Just as the economic conditions began to change, so the public's tastes began to shift also. The cultural mood of the early 1960s sprang in part from a desire among the 'baby boomer' post-war generation to break away from their parents' and grandparents' expectations. This sense of a need to find new ways of enjoying life extended to leisure time and, of course, to beer. By the 1960s the old-fashioned street-corner pubs, largely unchanged since the Victorian era, had a reputation as places where old men went to drink. Many were struggling and it was sometimes a relief to brewers when the demolition ball took away a failing, worthless property.

This was the era of the open-plan pub that did away with the traditional separate bar and lounge. New pubs, including

Higson's pub the Moby Dick, which opened in West Kirby on Wirral in 1964, were built along the lines of a large club, with a central bar, window seats and function rooms. The Moby Dick became a Higson's flagship and the design triggered a rash of pub refurbishments, most of which involved knocking out interior walls from old Victorian buildings. The arrival of lager in British pubs in the 1960s also helped to attract young drinkers, especially women, since 'real' ale was variable in quality and was in any case associated with old-fashioned tastes.

In an effort to attract younger drinkers away from their television sets at home, breweries also began to market the idea of the 'packaged pint'. Jukeboxes were installed to provide music and in some cases traditional pub games such as darts and dominoes took second place to televised sports, especially for major sporting events, such as the Wimbledon final or the Grand National. By the 1970s food had also found its way into many pubs with chicken in a basket, prawn cocktail and scampi heading the list of the decade's favourite bar meals.

Brewers ran advertising campaigns aimed at convincing younger drinkers that pubs might be interesting places to go. One Brewers' Society advertisement from 1966 shows the triumphant Bill Shankly Liverpool team sitting in a modern pub during the day, holding up half-finished pints and smiling at the camera with the caption 'Look in at the local'. The players, including Tommy Lawrence, Gerry Byrne and Ian St John, are clean-shaven young men in suits and ties. The text underneath the picture reads:

> They don't spend a lot of time in pubs, and when they go there they don't drink heavily. But the odd pint or shandy

means a lot to them ... 'the pub is a great place to unwind after you've been keyed up for a big match'.[82]

It was then considered normal for top-flight footballers to go to the pub on the day before an important local derby, but more significant is the message the picture puts across, that pubs were fashionable places where healthy young people could drink in moderation. This was a far cry from the seedy, down-at-heel image many pubs had at the time. Although fans of Everton might disagree, the well-dressed Liverpool football team in the picture offers an image of wholesome respectability that might also convince young women to 'look in at the local'.

Brewers in the 1960s and later worked hard to make their pubs appealing to the young, but this was another era of brewery mergers. By 1980, a handful of large companies controlled almost all of British brewing. One effect of this was to flatten out variations between pubs as they came under corporate control and competed for the same, limited market, but it also had a serious effect on regional and local variations in beers. 'Tied' houses sold only beers produced by the parent company and as the number of 'free' houses dwindled, beer drinkers found themselves with very little choice in what to drink.

As keg beers began to dominate the market, beer drinking became an exercise in corporate loyalty rather than an attachment to taste and quality. New production methods that halved the fermentation time to around four days and created a much more consistent product have been blamed for the almost total collapse of traditional brewing in the 1970s and 1980s. Higson's, which survived the frenzy

82 Gourvish and Wilson, *The British Brewing Industry*, plate 66.

of mergers and continued brewing its own range of beers until the 1980s, gave in to market forces and began planning an expansion of the brewery in the late 1970s. The main purpose of the expansion was to move into canning and the production of lager, including a keg lager for the pubs and the canned 'Prost' brand.

Higson's profits grew steadily in the 1960s and 1970s, though in some ways the company was slow to move with the times. It began producing keg beers, but its draught mild and bitter remained popular on Merseyside. Higson's also continued its tradition of imaginative and distinctively Liverpool advertising with a series of line-drawn cartoon characters with names such as 'Pierre Head' and 'Penny Lane' supping pints. The tagline was 'Real Liverpool Pubs, Real Liverpool Beer'. A comparison of the strength of beers brewed in this period show just how much the times, and the beer, had changed. In 1977 Higson's strongest brew, a barley wine known as 'Stingo', had an original gravity of 1080 degrees, while the pale ale came out at 1037 degrees and the draught bitter 1039. In the 1860s Robert Cain was brewing basic bitter ale at 1060 degrees and higher, while in the years before the First World War Guinness was measured at 1074 degrees, not far below 'Stingo' in the 1970s. Guinness, however, was sold by the pint; 'Stingo' was sold by the 'nip'.

Higson's expansion of the brewery in the late 1970s was the most significant development plan since Cain's own rebuilding almost a century before. Having won a contract to brew Kaltenberg lager under licence, the aim was to raise output at the Stanhope Street site to 160,000 barrels, a plan which included the installation of a new brewhouse between the old brewery building and Parliament Street. The foundation stone for the new brewhouse was laid by the Rt. Hon. Edward, Earl of Liverpool, in 1980 and two years later it was in production.

During the 1970s brewing became more like a branch of the chemical industry. Output and profit went before quality and the natural process of fermentation almost became an inconvenience. Brewers even experimented with 'continuous' production, a system that practically abandoned the idea of separate brews. Through their size the big firms had protected themselves from variations in the harvest, while technology and chemistry had turned beer into a uniform, reliable, but for the most part dull product.

The arrival of keg beer in the 1960s also had a negative effect on the quality of so-called real ales. One of the advantages of having beer stored and transported in pressurised kegs is that it makes the whole process easier and less time-consuming, both at the brewery and at the pub. Kegs removed the need for publicans to look after their beer in the cellar and as the old cellaring skills disappeared, so real ales became less well kept, less reliable and less popular. The recession that hit in the late 1970s, and persisted under the Thatcher government for most of the following decade, pushed traditional pubs, and traditional ales, into an almost terminal decline.

By the early 1980s the writing was on the wall for regional brewers such as Higson's. Although the company had avoided being caught up in the round of mergers that had transformed the industry over the previous twenty years, even a state-of-the-art brewhouse, an expanding distribution chain that included the Mellors off-licences, and a strong local brand could not save it from the big conglomerates. Building the new brewhouse had left the company overstretched and short of money, while local lager drinkers preferred continental brands to Higson's own offering. By 1985 Higson's was in need of help and it was bought by the Manchester brewer Boddington's.

After the Boddington's takeover Higson's continued to brew its own ales for a few years, but even a brand as well-known as Boddington's could not resist a takeover offer from a giant like Whitbread. When Boddington's was absorbed into the Whitbread empire in 1990 production of Higson's bitter and mild was transferred to Sheffield and the Stanhope Street site was used for canning and distribution. It looked for a while as if more than two centuries of brewing tradition on the site would come to an end. Especially for the occasion in 1990, Higson's produced a bottled beer it called 'The Last Drop'.

By 1989 Liverpool itself was in a sorry state. Battered by recession, by more than two decades of labour disputes, political battles and urban strife, the city had a reputation for crime, unemployment and failure. In the late 1970s unemployment among adults under 24 stood at around 50 per cent and on the estates along the docks conditions were little better than they had been in the nineteenth century. Children were malnourished, ill-health was the norm and people went without basic necessities such as clothes and shoes. For non-whites the problem of finding work was even worse. A form of unofficial segregation meant that most of the black population lived in Liverpool 8, once the centre of Liverpool's cultural life and by then a ghetto.

Liverpool's racial and community divisions had been ignored for decades. The old antagonism between Catholics and Protestants continued to plague many of the housing estates, while the black population rebelled against police and community prejudice. The extent of the problem, which was no doubt made worse by poverty and absolute despera- tion, was not formally recognised until 1980, when the city council established a Race Relations Liaison Committee. Then in July 1981 the Toxteth riots erupted. What began as a dispute between a black man, Leroy Alphonse Cooper, and the police soon turned into large-scale public disorder. It is estimated that in the two weeks of violence and looting around 500 buildings were damaged or destroyed by fire at a cost of £11 million, and one person died. The rioting implanted Liverpool in the national consciousness as an urban wasteland divided along racial lines.

In a political atmosphere of confrontation and harsh economic discipline many believed that the city was being punished by the Thatcher government for its dependency on government support and its failure to reform. Attempts at regeneration had been made, including the restoration of the Albert Dock, and the first International Garden Festival in 1984, which temporarily transformed an area of urban decay into a showcase for garden design. But Liverpool's tradition of going its own way worked against it. The Garden Festival did nothing to alleviate the deep poverty visible in the city and for many it became an emblem of the Tory government's contempt for Northern towns. As the rest of the country moved towards the Conservatives, Liverpool, historically a Conservative working-class stronghold, swung sharply to the left in the late 1970s and stayed there throughout the 1980s.

By the time the Thatcher government came to power in 1979 the ineffective Liverpool Labour Party was being taken over by its 'Militant Tendency' and in 1983, with pledges to build new council housing and create jobs, Labour took control of the city. The most popular pledge of all, though, was the promise to confront the government. Derek Hatton, the deputy leader of the Labour group, became a bogeyman for the Thatcher government, for the press and for the national leadership of his own party. His insistence on continuing to spend money on social and cultural projects went directly against the government's attempts to cut back on public spending and almost bankrupted the city.

The confrontational politics of the 1980s did not help with rebuilding communities or with the city's image in the country. Carla Lane's hugely popular television comedy series *Bread*, which aired between 1986 and 1991, poked fun at Liverpool's image as a place where people lived on state benefits and showed no sign of wanting to work. The series featured the Boswells, a large Catholic-Irish family of lovable rogues, and was criticised in Liverpool because it exploited unkind popular stereotypes of the city. The Boswells quickly became national favourites and although they did nothing to promote Liverpool as a modern, forward-looking city, their resilience and self-confidence were aspects of the city that could be seen on the streets.

Even in the depths of the recession the people of Liverpool had reasons to celebrate. Their two football teams dominated the English game in the 1970s and 1980s while the Grand National enjoyed a resurgence in popularity after the successes of Red Rum, who won the race for the third time in 1977. Besides Carla Lane, Liverpool writers who enjoyed national acclaim included Alan Bleasdale, whose *Boys from the Black Stuff* had a major impact when it aired in 1982, and Willy Russell, whose *Blood Brothers* and *Shirley Valentine* have proved among the most enduring stories of their generation. Phil Redmond, whose soap *Brookside* was one of the most popular British television shows of the 1980s and 1990s, brought a little Scouse grit to an otherwise bland genre. Liverpool comics from Kenny Everett to Alexei Sayle continued to demonstrate the city's remarkable talent for hard-edged humour.

The year 1989 was to prove the low point in Liverpool's self-esteem, but it also marked the beginnings of a slow revival. On 15 April 1989 the FA Cup semi-final between Liverpool FC and Nottingham Forest was the backdrop for one of English football's darkest tragedies. At Sheffield Wednesday's Hillsborough ground 96 Liverpool fans were killed in a crush caused by police blunders that allowed far too many people into the stadium. As the city mourned, Liverpool fans were accused of stealing from the dead. Jon Murden sums up the significance of the reaction of the press to Liverpool's loss:

> *The Sun* newspaper printed the vilest pack of lies, castigating the people of Liverpool ... The very fact that [elements of the media] felt it acceptable to make such comments in the wake of such a tragedy gives some indication of the depths to which Liverpool's stock had sunk.[83]

This was the point at which Liverpool acquired its reputation as a maudlin, self-pitying city. It was also the point at which the revival began.

In 1990, after Whitbread's takeover of Boddington's, Robert Cain's brewery came up for sale. It was bought by GB Breweries, run by John Hughes. Hughes had experience

---

83 Murden, 'City of Change and Challenge', p. 470.

of selling soft drinks to the supermarkets and when the brewery re-opened it was to brew supermarket own-brand canned beers. Then in 1991, after a break of seventy years and with the country in the grip of yet another recession, Robert Cain's brewery began producing cask ales under the Robert Cain name.

The revival of an old Liverpool brand at a time when the seeds of regeneration were being sown in the city was an important event. In response to lobbying by the Campaign for Real Ale (CAMRA) and the few remaining small regional brewers, the Monopolies and Mergers Commission had demanded legislation to force the big brewers to open up their pubs to smaller breweries. The 1989 'Beer Orders' legislation freed 11,000 pubs from their ties to the brewers and required them to offer at least one 'guest beer'. Emerging from the shadow of the big brewing companies Cain's cask-conditioned ale, known as Cain's Traditional Bitter, was relaunched in March 1991. The first pint was drunk by Lord Charles 'Charlie' Brocket, the great-great-grandson of Robert Cain.

Soon after GB Breweries relaunched the Cain's brand the company was taken over by the Danish brewing company, Bryggerigruppen A/S, famous for its Faxe brand. The Danish company clearly saw potential in both the brewery and the Cain's brand and, hoping to build on the new openness in the pub trade, injected substantial amounts of cash for development. Steve Holt, who had revived the Cain's name when he took over as manager of the brewery, developed a range of traditional ales and branding that built on Robert Cain's own image as a Victorian gentleman. One of William Daniels' portraits of Cain became a familiar sight around

Liverpool, the brewer's assertive and self-confident stare proclaiming Cain's as 'The Great Merseyside Tradition'.

Holt's interest in the brewery and its history stretched as far as exploring the underground lake beneath the site, and to refurbishing the old hop store at the top of the building. Cain's bitter in particular became a Liverpool favourite and as the 1990s progressed Cain's once again became part of the city's social fabric. But even though Cain's was once again a familiar sight in Liverpool's pubs, the brewery was barely operating as a business in its own right. Over the course of the decade the Danish parent company poured an estimated £10 million into Robert Cain's brewery, keeping the name alive despite heavy losses.

Like Liverpool itself, which had developed tentatively in the 1990s, the Cain's brand was viewed positively, but it was too weak to survive without a new approach. In the 1970s and 1980s poor-quality keg beers had damaged the reputation of brewers and the whole brewing industry. Part of re-establishing that reputation was an effort to look back to a period in which brewers had been trustworthy figures producing quality beer and supporting traditional values. Men like Robert Cain had a reputation for firm but fair dealing in his business and private life, while his beer more than lived up to its billing as 'superior ale'. But looking backward was not what Cain's or Liverpool needed. It was not until the century ended that the city really began to think about what it wanted to be rather than what it had been long ago.

9

Full Circle

In 1887, when he was at his peak as a brewer, an entrepreneur and a man of influence, Robert Cain offered this advice to would-be entrepreneurs:

> The great thing is in being able to recognise an improvement when you see it. But a man who is to be successful, when he does see an improvement, begins at once to strain every nerve and to take the risk of carrying it out. If a man remains quite satisfied with what he has and is always afraid and nervous of laying out money in this way, and has no ambition to go ahead, he is not only stationary but begins to be so far outstripped by more enterprising rivals that he ultimately finds himself out of the hunt altogether.[84]

This is the essence of Robert Cain's approach to business and to life: to take opportunities where they come, to 'strain every nerve' in carrying out improvements, and not to be afraid of doing so. But as the last fireworks of the millennium celebrations fell back into the Mersey, Cain's advice rang hollow. During the 1990s Liverpool had seen some new development. The Museum of Liverpool Life opened in 1993 and Paul McCartney's Liverpool Institute for Performing Arts was founded in 1996. But progress was slow and while

84 *Liverpool Review*, 17 September 1887, p. 10.

regeneration projects for the city were planned, not far from the main streets boarded-up shops and crumbling warehouses told a different story of poverty and decay. The economic recovery of the late 1990s faltered as the new century began, and faced with mounting losses the Danish parent company considered the future of the brewery and the Cain's brand.

By then the brewery was losing in the region of £2 million a year and before long the news was out in the city that it was in trouble. It was impossible for brewing alone to cover those kinds of losses, but a campaign was set up to urge drinkers to buy Cain's beer and show support. It didn't work, and by late summer 2001 the parent company had decided that enough was enough. Brewing stopped and the brewery was put up for sale. Just as Liverpool seemed to be recovering from decades of neglect and division it looked as if it would finally lose its brewery.

What happened next is a story typical of Liverpool and a classic tale of modern Britain. As Christmas 2001 approached the sale of Cain's brewery came to the attention of two brothers, Ajmail and Sudarghara Dusanj. They were entrepreneurs who over the previous few years had turned around the ailing Gardner-Shaw soft drinks firm in the West Midlands. Sudarghara, the older of the two, was born in 1965, and his brother Ajmail in 1966, in Chatham, Kent. Their father, Surinder, who arrived in Britain from the Punjab in 1962, was part of a wave of immigration from India, Pakistan and the West Indies that helped sustain Britain's economy in the 1950s and 1960s.

Like economic migrants from earlier times Surinder Dusanj worked as a labourer, in his case on construction projects such as the M1 motorway, the Dungeness nuclear power station, and in a foundry. Surinder Dusanj could not speak English when he arrived in England aged 23. By the late 1970s, with the country in turmoil and his two sons growing up fast, he realised he had to do something to secure a living for his family. In 1983, with money he had saved over the previous twenty years, and from re-mortgaging the family home, he bought a chip shop in Chatham for £35,000 and became a businessman.

Sudarghara and Ajmail helped in the shop after school and by the time they were leaving college in 1986 the family had bought a convenience store and then an off-licence. They expanded the business by buying failed high-street shops and converting them to takeaways and later newsagents and off-licences. But the family found it difficult to manage more than four shops at any one time. Beyond that number the separate businesses became difficult to control. In all, between 1987 and 1992 the Dusanj family ran nine shops, buying them cheap, building up the business, then selling them on to relatives.

The brothers had taken business courses at Dartford College in Kent and the shops had been a valuable source of experience. But by the early 1990s they were looking for a new challenge. In 1992 they were running their own newsagents' shops and would spend their time scanning the papers in between customers. A story in the *Financial Times* about Gardner-Shaw going into receivership caught their eye. They thought that if they could run a company from one place there would be more opportunity to develop and expand. The pair admit that at the time they had no real management experience, but this looked like the 'next step' and they learned fast. With help from their father they sold everything and bought the troubled soft drinks firm.

Moving north was a risk. The brothers joked about how they felt: 'The first day we arrived at Gardner-Shaw we realised what a huge risk it was. ... If there had been a get-out clause we would have taken it.' But it didn't take long for them to work out what to do. The first step was to rebuild the brand. Gardner-Shaw sold traditional soft drinks in return-able glass bottles, but within a matter of months the Dusanjs had introduced new lines and diversified into supplying pubs and off-licences. Soon they had distribution centres around the West Midlands, had added beer and spirits to the range, and had raised the annual turnover from £450,000 to £8 million. By 2001 they had begun to sense that it was time to move on to a bigger challenge, and the following spring they bought Cain's brewery for around £3.5 million.

In Liverpool in early 2002 it was feared the Cain's brewery would be closed down for good. When several bidders expressed an interest the feeling in the city was that asset strippers would sell it off bit by bit. Nobody was really sure what the Dusanj brothers would do with the brewery, but right from the start they threw themselves into reviving the brand and rebuilding Cain's as a modern, innovative craft brewer. They have said on many occasions since that this was a once-in-a-lifetime opportunity and one they could not pass up. With experience of the packing and distribution side of the brewing business and with an intuitive sense of how Cain's could be saved, the brothers took on the brewery with an eye to the long term.

At first the brewery workers were unsure about their future, especially when restructuring meant that 30 employees were laid off. But the Dusanjs quickly earned their trust with their enthusiasm, passion and willingness to work. As they saw it they were 'just two guys with no money' trying to make the brewery a success. And unlike the Gardner-Shaw experience, Cain's was a challenge they relished and understood from the start. They knew the value of the brewery to the city and that they were committing themselves to developing it as a going concern. Most of those early weeks were spent establishing a relationship with the workers and with making their intentions known. Their informal and straight-talking attitude, together with their ambitious plans, could hardly fail to win over the people of Liverpool. And their acceptance was marked in true Scouse style; it wasn't long before they had been renamed Bill and Sid by the brewery workers.

Although they had a working brewery, a known brand and a solid product, the Dusanjs knew that the mindset of the company was holding it back. The Robert Cain brewery, one of Liverpool's best-loved buildings, had been at the heart of a brewing empire at a time when Liverpool itself was a powerful and wealthy city. The fortunes of local brands such as Cain's can make a real impact on the atmosphere and mood of a place and the revival of the brewery at the hands of ambitious and confident entrepreneurs went some way towards changing the mindset of Liverpool itself. The fact that the company's new owners were not from Liverpool also says a great deal about the city's openness and willingness to 'see an improvement' when it comes along. But for years the brewery and the city had struggled and a culture of survival and 'getting by' had set in.

After 2002 new branding emphasised Robert Cain's forward-looking values while remembering the remarkable heritage of the city and the brewery. Out went the old logos and in came a fresher design. Daniels' glowering portrait of Cain, which had been used in advertising during the 1990s, was replaced with a silhouette of the founder. This kept Robert Cain and his achievement at the centre, but also suggested that the past was no longer staring down the present. Delicately drawn hops curled their way around the lettering of the Cain's name. In the twenty-first century the brewery would return to the idea of brewing as a natural process, focusing on quality ingredients and care.

The introduction of a continental-style lager is a case in point. As a result of Higson's expansion, the brewhouse was designed for brewing lager, with a mash converter and lauter tun, which separates the grains from the wort, rather than a traditional mash tun. So Cain's Finest Lager, first produced in 2004, seemed a good addition to the growing range, which included a bitter, mild and IPA, and specials, such as the award-winning Raisin Beer. As Higson's and other regional brewers found out, the lager market is a difficult one, but as lager drinkers themselves, the Dusanjs were better placed than most to understand it.

Brewed with malt made from Maris Otter barley, generally thought to be the best malting barley in the world, Cain's Finest Lager was the first ever British premium lager. The Dusanj brothers joked that they started in the chip shop with Maris Piper potatoes so Maris Otter barley was the obvious choice. On the advice of beer writer Roger Protz, the beer was to be 'lagered' in the traditional way for three months before being released for sale, adding to the flavour and aroma. Not long after its launch, in 2005 the men's style magazine GQ voted Cain's Finest Lager number two in its list of '100 best things in the world' and called it 'the greatest bottled lager'. Even CAMRA, an organisation that began partly as a reaction against traditional British breweries turning to lager brewing, celebrated the achievement. Building on that success, in April 2007 Cain's brewed a 'Birthday Bock' to celebrate Liverpool's 800th birthday and the birth month of Robert Cain.

By entering a market in which no British brewers had ever succeeded before, the Dusanjs took an important step in their attempt to reach a wider market and become brewers of beer from Liverpool, rather than just for Liverpool. As part of the effort to become 'Britain's favourite brewer' they began to develop the Cain's brand in a more up-to-date way. The release of Cain's distinctive Wheat Beer in the autumn of 2007 confirmed the brewery as one of Britain's most modern producers of high-quality beers.

While the Dusanjs were settling in to their new surroundings, in 2002 the city had plans to bid for the coveted European Capital of Culture title. Slow but steady progress was being made in the regeneration of Liverpool's city centre and there was a sense that like other post-industrial Northern cities, such as Manchester and Newcastle, Liverpool could begin to look again to the future. In 2003, when the culture secretary Tessa Jowell announced that Liverpool had won the competition, many voices claimed that Merseyside was undeserving of the honour. Other cities, Newcastle included, protested that Liverpool was hardly one of Britain's cultural centres and as a European city Liverpool also seemed unsuitable. In 2003 an Atlantic-facing attitude was deeply unfashionable and just three years earlier Liverpool had shared millennium celebrations with New York. Nevertheless, as novelist Linda Grant wrote in *The Guardian* soon after the announcement,

'If the city can be reborn, this is its moment'.[85]

The image of Liverpool as 'sailortown', lacking an interest or investment in culture, was, of course, highly inaccurate and unfair. Liverpool's past as a city celebrated for its art, music, literature and arts patronage made it an ideal candidate for reinvention in the years leading up to 2008 and beyond. The Dusanj brothers also saw this as an opportunity for the brewery to reconnect with the city. Reviving Robert Cain's own interest in the arts they made a successful bid for Cain's to become the official beer of the Capital of Culture in 2008, beating off larger competitors in the process. The brewery invested £1 million in Capital of Culture plans and took its connection with the arts further in 2006 when Cain's became the official supplier of beer to the Tate art galleries in Liverpool, London and St Ives.

By then the brewery had won many awards, beginning in 2003 with supermarket chain Tesco's Best Beer Award. Cain's Raisin Beer won plaudits for innovation from the Californian raisin industry and picked up CAMRA's prestigious 'Beer of the Festival' award at the Liverpool Beer Festival in 2004. Cain's Finest Lager won a string of awards from CAMRA and elsewhere, while other beers have been honoured by organisations such as the Society of Independent Brewers. Since 2002 the remarkable turnaround of Cain's has also been noted by business leaders. The Dusanj brothers won the Business and Commerce prize at the Asian Jewel Awards in 2004, the year the brewery edged back into profit. A few months earlier they were named 'Corporate Players of the Year' for 2003 by North West Business Insider magazine. In

85 Linda Grant, 'History broke Liverpool, and it broke my heart', *The Guardian*, 5 June 2003.

2005 they were named Directors of the Year by the Institute of Directors.

Cain's brewery is one of Liverpool's best-loved buildings and represents the city's past as a powerhouse of Victorian industry and trade. In the twenty-first century it has also become an emblem of revival, ambition and independent spirit, qualities for which Liverpool was once famous. By the time Liverpool came to celebrate its 800th anniversary in 2007, Cain's was central to the way the city saw itself. Even though it had almost disappeared altogether just five years before, the brewery was once again an institution that seemed solid and unbreakable; a forward-looking brand in a city that needed to build for the future.

As the Capital of Culture year came into sight through a fog of political in-fighting and bruised egos, the Dusanj brothers had expansion in mind. They negotiated a takeover deal with Honeycombe Leisure PLC, a company that ran a chain of pubs and hotels across the North West. Although Honeycombe was the larger company it was struggling in difficult trading conditions, soon to be made worse by a ban on smoking in public places that came into force in July 2007. Although welcomed by the majority of non-smokers, for whom pub visits became a much more pleasant experience, the smoking ban forced publicans to make arrangements for many of their customers to drink and smoke outside even in bad weather. It was a factor in declining beer sales in pubs during 2007 and 2008.

The 'reverse takeover' of Honeycombe, which was completed on 7 June 2007, saw the Dusanjs take a controlling interest in the merged organisation, which became known as the Cains Beer Company PLC. In the process they acquired over 100 pubs, inns and hotels around North-West England, to go with the 11 already held by Cain's in Liverpool itself. A Bank of Scotland statement after the deal was agreed in May said:

> Bank of Scotland is delighted to be supporting a highly reputable and well-known local business with national ambitions to make its mark with the UK brewery sector. Throughout the course of our discussions with Cains, we've been consistently impressed by the strong management demonstrated by the Dusanj brothers. Their entrepreneurial aspirations for the business closely reflect Bank of Scotland's own commitment to funding ambitious and fast-growing companies throughout the UK.

With the Robert Cain brewery as its centre of operations the new company had a turnover of £65 million and, although the Honeycombe side of the operation was lossmaking, the prospects for the new company were such that bankers were willing to lend £40 million to support its business plan, three quarters of which was a loan facility to see Cain's through the years following the merger.

One advantage of the deal was that it brought Cain's to the stock market for the first time, an achievement that the brothers have described as the most significant of their lives up to that date. With a market capitalisation of around £7.5 million and a total value of around £37 million, the new enlarged company raised £5 million for new investment and expansion. In November the same year Cain's also celebrated the global success of its innovative Raisin Beer, which was named the World's Best Fruit Beer at the 2007 International Beer Awards.

It is an indication of the popularity of Cain's and its position as a producer of high-quality real ales that the

CAMRA Members Investment Club was a strong supporter of the move. CAMRA members bought over a million shares in the new company, something that would have been almost unimaginable twenty years earlier. This was the secret behind the success of the brewery after 2002. Through its quality cask and bottled beers, through its canned super-market own-brand lines, and through operating as a canning and bottling facility for other quality brewers, the brewery could operate in many different markets, drawing support from beer drinkers of all kinds. Just as it did under the founder in the 1860s the brewery reached people across the city and beyond. By the end of 2007 the achievement of the Dusanj brothers in rescuing the brewery and rebuilding the brand had made them heroes in Liverpool. Their progress was also widely admired in the brewing industry, especially among smaller 'craft' brewers who shared their enthusiasm for creating new, innovative beers.

But even as the company floated on the Alternative Investment Market in the summer of 2007, economic storm clouds were gathering. Newcastle-based bank Northern Rock found itself over-exposed to so-called 'sub-prime' mortgages and in September it asked for help from the Bank of England to stay in business. This proved to be a sign of difficult times ahead for everyone. As what became known as the 'credit crunch' increased in pressure, banks became less willing to lend money and by the time Northern Rock was taken over by the government in February 2008 the financial climate had changed completely. With over 100 pubs in need of refurbishment and maintenance, the Cains Beer Company depended on the goodwill of its bankers and although it did not seem like a problem at the time of the merger, the company's borrowing would later prove to be its downfall.

Through the autumn of 2007 and into the following spring the Dusanj brothers worked on a plan to improve the former Honeycombe pubs and get Cain's beers into supermarkets around Britain. There was some opposition to the way the new company was run, especially among former Honeycombe publicans who were used to supplying guest beers from several different breweries. Many disliked having to offer only Cain's beers to their customers and pointed out that it was because Cain's beers had themselves been offered as guest ales that the brewery had been able to survive. The Dusanjs also came in for criticism from former Honeycombe managers and other employees who resented their experience being overlooked and felt that the refurbishment plan amounted to little more than an exercise in rebranding. Even so, in the second half of 2007 the expansion was generally seen as a positive thing both for the company and for Liverpool.

What nobody foresaw, however, was a global economic crisis that by the autumn of 2008 would bring the world banking system to its knees and threaten to plunge Western economies into recession on a scale not seen for generations. Even in the days of Robert Cain, brewing was exposed to global markets – Cain himself bought hops from Germany and malt made from Californian barley – but in 2007 this had become even more important. Commodity prices began to rise sharply, adding to problems in the brewing industry caused by rising taxes and falling beer sales. In the first half of 2008 the price of cereals soared, the price of oil and gas rose dramatically, while at the same time drinkers tightened their belts and began to stay at home.

In May 2008 a trading statement for the Cains Beer
Company noted the difficult conditions and on 28 July the
Cains Beer Company interim report was released, covering
the six months up to April 2008. The report was upbeat
about rising beer sales in supermarkets and about the possibility of making good on the original business plan. But it
also recorded half-yearly losses of £4.5 million to add to
the £2.7 million in losses for the 14 months up to October
2007. While the company was far from going bust it was
very short of funds. It also emerged that the company faced
a winding-up order imposed by HM Revenue and Customs
in a dispute over an unpaid tax bill. Suddenly, and almost
without warning, Cain's was in trouble again.

To make matters worse, by the time the company's credit
facility came up for renewal in July its banker, the Bank of
Scotland, was having problems of its own. Negotiations took
place throughout July to secure funding for the Cains Beer
Company, but on 1 August the bank finally refused to extend
its credit. During this period Ajmail Dusanj agreed that the
situation was not unlike Robert Cain's own early struggles.
But Cain's Victorian optimism did not match up with the
reality of the brewing industry in 2008. Cain's lacked funds
to continue operating and on 7 August administrators from
PricewaterhouseCoopers were called in to take charge of the
business and try to save at least some of the 1,000 jobs. The
brewery was up for sale again.

In Liverpool there was a sense of shock that this could
happen. Cain's had become a symbol of Liverpool's rebirth,
and enthusiasm for the home-grown brewery had been
matched by a growing confidence in the place as a twenty-
first-century city. Almost inevitably the collapse of Cain's

was seen in some quarters as a sign of Liverpool's own overconfidence. Yet within days of administrators moving in and the Dusanj brothers moving out, several companies were tipped to buy the brewery, including the Burton brewer Marstons and a Scottish management group, MMSI, which had bought the Isle of Arran Brewery under similar circumstances earlier in the year. Sudarghara Dusanj went on the record to tell the *Liverpool Daily Post*: 'We are hopeful. It's a good brewery and a good business.' After months of struggling to find funding, neither he nor his brother could accept that the brewery was finished.

As administrators began to shut down pubs, including the popular Ship Inn or 'Blood Tub' at Lathom in West Lancashire and the Thatch Inn in Southport, the brewery kept working. It became clear that while the Cains Beer Company was in trouble, the brewery itself was still a going concern. Despite serious problems for brewing in 2007 and 2008 many small regional breweries, including Moorhouses in Burnley, managed to expand production. In fact locally brewed real ale looked set to buck the national trend of falling beer sales and Cain's looked a good prospect for the right buyer. Marstons, itself a large group, was committed to maintaining separate breweries for the brands under its ownership, seeing the value in keeping local brands such as Jennings of Cumbria, Brakspear of Oxfordshire and Ringwood of Hampshire based in their communities. Cain's, with its strong local ties and powerful branding, was too valuable to be allowed to die. MMSI even promised that if Cain's folded they would set up a brewery of their own in the city, emphasising the point that regional brewing could be a good business proposition even in difficult times.

The uncertainties lingered on through August and September, and it emerged that the Dusanj family had a trump card up its sleeve. Back in 2002, when Cain's was rescued from closure, the Dusanjs had put the brewery and the nine Liverpool pubs they bought with it into a family trust. Their reason for doing so was to protect themselves and the wider family from the loss of the business, but having control of the freehold on the brewery site and its core pubs meant the Dusanj brothers could influence the terms of any sale to a third party. Despite losing control of the company, they remained powerful players in the fight to save it and by mid-September they looked likely to buy back the business and regain control of the brewery.

The Dusanj brothers finally managed to negotiate a deal with the administrators late on 21 September and their success was announced in the *Daily Post* the following day. For brewery workers there were sighs of relief that their jobs had been secured, but the overall reaction around Liverpool was rather subdued. After 43 days of uncertainty, during which the brothers had been criticised for the mistake they made in taking over Honeycombe, the sheen had come off the previous six years of expansion and awards. In a climate of financial crisis and looming recession, when rich city bankers were being rewarded for failure with multi-million-pound 'golden parachutes', the idea that the Dusanj brothers could take back a company they had pushed to the brink of disaster did not go down especially well. The deal itself, while not at all unfair in the world of business, was seen by some as unjustifiable, especially when newspapers reported that the sale of the company to other bidders had been soured by the brothers' demands for rent of £1 million a year.

After many days of long and exhausting negotiations the Dusanj brothers made an uncharacteristically low-key statement through a spokesman, reported by the *Daily Post*: 'They have been working hard to try to make sure they can protect jobs and carry on Cain's brewery. As time goes by, they will be more inclined to speak personally about what's happened and their future plans.'[86] This was very different from the confident start they had made in 2002 and a long way from the chirpy 'Bill and Sid' image cultivated as they became part of the Cain's mythology. The summer's events had given them an experience of business that they had never seen before and changed forever their relationship with the city of Liverpool. It was perhaps understandable that this would be a sober affair.

For Liverpool, rocked by the news of Cain's collapse in August, the summer of 2008 will also be remembered for the European Capital of Culture celebrations. In 2008 Liverpool made the headlines mainly for its art, not its brewery. From concerts and art exhibitions to street theatre and a spectacular giant spider, Liverpool showed the world what it had to offer and put on a show it could be proud of. The brewery Robert Cain built while Liverpool found its feet in the nineteenth century remains one of the city's great institutions. From its rescue in 2002 the revival of Cain's and the work of the Dusanj brothers in promoting the city and its beer were a key factor in Liverpool's growing self-confidence and pride. But great institutions, like great cities, are bigger than the people who look after them and they need to nurtured, fought for and defended. As Liverpool decides how to build on the Capital of Culture year, its great

86 *Daily Post*, 22 September 2008.

brewery faces a difficult period of recovery. Robert Cain, the gentleman brewer born in poverty and raised in the slums, knew a thing or two about struggle and persistence. His words of encouragement sum up the challenges ahead for the brewery and the city:

> While everyone is against you, while you are unknown, suspected, weak in credit – those are the troublesome days. If a man has the strength and foresight to live through this and keep a foothold he will find the next stages perhaps as hard in work but more encouraging as regards profits and prospects.[87]

87 *Liverpool Review*, 17 September 1887, p. 10.

Timeline

1790–1839

1796

James Cain, the father of Robert Cain, born in County Monahan, Ireland.

1798

Irish uprising, assisted by the French and led by Wolfe Tone, fails to overthrow the British occupation of Ireland.

1807

Abolition of slave trade in the British Empire. Liverpool turns to cotton as its primary trading commodity.

1820

James Cain, an itinerant labourer, enlists in the 88th Regiment of Foot 'Connaught Rangers' at Chester. At about this time he marries RC's mother, Mary.

1821

Birth of Hannah Cain, RC's older sister.

1826

29 April. RC born on Spike Island, County Cork, Ireland.

Engineer George Stephenson begins building the Liverpool to Manchester Railway. When it opened in 1830 it was the first passenger railway in the world.

1827

10 November. RC's father discharged from the army. Soon afterwards the family move to Liverpool to find work.

1832

A cholera epidemic in Liverpool kills 1,523 people and infects many thousands more.

1840–1849

1840

The (Royal) Liverpool Philharmonic Society is founded. Samuel Cunard begins a twice-weekly passenger service from Liverpool to the Eastern United States.

1841

The Cain family, a total of seven people, live in a court dwelling off Bent Street. The family included Hannah and her husband Pierce Reddy who had been married the year before as well as Robert, his sister Mary (b. 1828) and his brother William (b. 1839).

1841–1847 *(approx.)*

RC serving an apprenticeship as a cooper on the dangerous West African palm oil trade route.

1847

4 April. RC marries 17-year-old Ann Newall at St Philip's Church, Hardman Street.

Irish immigration to Liverpool peaks at almost 300,000 in a single year. The year became known as Black '47.

As public health deteriorates Liverpool becomes the centre for a public health movement. The Liverpool Sanitary Act is passed and Liverpool appoints the first Medical Officer for Health anywhere in the world. The first person to hold the post is Dr Duncan.

1848

Birth of Robert James Cain, RC's first son (d. 1909).

1850–1869

1850

RC purchases a small brewery on Limekiln Lane. Continues to work as a journeyman cooper. Birth of Hannah Cain (d. 1874).

1853

Birth of Mary Cain (d. 1931).

1854–1856

The Crimean War opens up new opportunities for Liverpool's steamship companies to exploit trade in the Mediterranean.

1854

RC buys a larger brewery on Wilton Street and doubles his output. The Limekiln Lane brewery is leased to another brewer.

1856

Birth of Alfred Dean Cain (d. 1899).
David Lewis founds his revolutionary department store. The first water from Rivington Pike arrives in Liverpool. People are suspicious of its dark, peat colouring, but the water is at least clean.

1858

RC buys the Stanhope Street 'Mersey Brewery' from the Hindley family.

1859

Birth of Sarah Ann Cain.

1860

Robert Cain is owner and licensee of the Transatlantic Hotel on Stanhope Street and runs the hotel at the same time as the nearby brewery. Birth of Maria Cain (d. 1863). Opening of William Brown's Free Museum and Library.

1861–1865

The American Civil War leaves Liverpool shipping lines in control of Atlantic trade. Liverpool's willingness to work with the Southern states and even build warships for the Confederate cause puts it out of step with most other British cities.

1863

Birth of Lena Alexandra Cain.

1864

Birth of William Ernest Cain, who became joint chairman of Walker-Cain, and was a governor of Liverpool University. He received a knighthood in 1917 and became Baronet Cain in 1920 (d. 1924).

1864–1872 *(approx.)*

The Cain family live at 'Mersey View', Grassendale Park.

1866

Birth of Charles Alexander Cain (later Nall-Cain), who became joint chairman of Walker-Cain, was made a

baronet in 1924 and entered the House of Lords as Lord
Brocket in 1933 (d. 1934).
Cholera outbreak in Liverpool, though sanitation and
water supplies are improving.

1868
Birth of Herbert Cain (d. 1905).

1870–1889

1871
26 December. Death of James Cain, RC's father. Death
certificate witnessed by Pierce Reddy, his son-in-law.
Soon afterwards RC and his family move to 'Barn Hey',
a mansion in three acres of land on Aigburth Road. The
following year nearby Sefton Park opens and becomes a
focus for the city's wealthy merchants who build their
houses in the area.

1873
The Cain family entertains the painter William Daniels
at 'Barn Hey'. Daniels paints at least two portraits of
Robert Cain.

1874
Birth of Gertrude Amy Cain.

1877
Opening of the Walker Art Gallery.

1878
Everton FC is founded from the St Domingo's Methodist
Youth Club to play at Anfield. Fourteen years later in
1892 the club moves to Goodison Park and Liverpool FC
is founded to take its place at Anfield.

1880

Liverpool becomes a diocese of the Church of England and thus achieves city status. The following year a royal charter is signed creating a university college, now the University of Liverpool.

1886

Opening of the underground passenger railway across the Mersey from Liverpool to Birkenhead.

1887

Work begins on a large-scale expansion of the Stanhope Street brewery that would take three years to complete. At the same time The Albion pub is rebuilt and named The Central Hotel.

RC featured in *The Liverpool Review* as one of Liverpool's most successful men.

1890–1909

1893

The Liverpool Overhead Railway is opened, linking Dingle to Seaforth.

1896

12 March. Death of RC's wife Ann.

December. The brewery is incorporated and becomes Robert Cain and Sons Ltd. Soon afterwards RC moves to Hoylake to live in a huge mansion called 'Barn Hey', like the house on Aigburth Road.

1898

Approval given for the rebuilding of The Philharmonic Hotel on the corner of Hardman Street and Hope Street.

The new building is one of the finest public houses ever built and soon becomes a Liverpool landmark. It was built partly in response to the temperance campaign.

1902

Completion of major work at the brewery, extending and developing it for the new century.

1904

Work begins on Liverpool's Anglican Cathedral to a design by Giles Gilbert Scott. It was consecrated in 1924, but would not be completed until 1978.

1907

19 July. Death of Robert Cain. His funeral takes place on 22 July, attended by his surviving children and his nephew, James Reddy. A crowd of 3,000 people press at the gates of St James's cemetery and have to be restrained by the police.

Completion of The Vines public house. Like The Philharmonic it also incorporates decorative work by some of Liverpool's best craftsmen and designers.

August. Liverpool celebrates its 700th anniversary.

1909

Eleanor Rathbone becomes the first woman councillor.

1910–1929

1914–1918

World War I sees German submarines patrol the Irish Sea and Liverpool shipping under threat in the Atlantic.

1921

Robert Cain and Sons Ltd merges with Peter Walker

and Sons Ltd. Charles and William Cain head the new
company.

1923

Brewery building bought by Daniel Higson Ltd. The
Higson's name is added to the brewery walls soon afterwards.

1930–1949

1932

The population of Liverpool is thought to peak at
870,000.

1939–45

Liverpool is one of the key strategic ports for Allied
operations in World War II. It is the operational centre in
the Battle of the Atlantic, berthing around 1,300 convoys
of up to 60 ships each during this period.

1941

8–15 May. In the Liverpool Blitz over 50,000 people are
made homeless, 1,200 are seriously injured and 1,700
are killed. In order to sustain morale the severity of the
bombing is not reported.

1950–1969

1952

Work begins on the Kirkby estate and almost two decades
of slum clearance begins with the movement of 50,000
people into 10,000 new houses. Between 1966 and 1972
a further 38,000 families are moved to new residential
areas such as Cantril Farm and Netherley.

1955

Labour wins control of the city council for the first time

1956

The Overhead Railway, known as 'the dockers' umbrella', is closed and later dismantled. The following year Liverpool's trams are also closed down.

1957

John Lennon forms the Quarrymen, later to become known as the Beatles. In the decade that follows Liverpool bands dominate pop music and 'Merseybeat' becomes known around the world.

1962

Surinder Dusanj, father of the future owners of the Robert Cain brewery, arrives in Britain from the Punjab.

1968

Publication of the poetry anthology *The Mersey Sound* makes poets Roger McGough, Adrian Henri and Brian Patten famous. It also starts a national revival in the popularity of poetry.

1970–1989

1971

The Kingsway Tunnel, the second road tunnel under the Mersey, opens.

1978–85

Liverpool is among the most severely affected cities as the country slips into recession. Containerisation a decade before had led to the loss of thousands of jobs and now Liverpool's manufacturing firms collapse with the loss of 40,000 more. Unemployment peaks at 25 per cent, but in certain parts of the city more than half the working population have no paid work.

1981

Merseyside Development Corporation is formed to promote regeneration. By now around 12,000 people are leaving the city each year.

Three days of rioting in Toxteth are triggered by police harassment as black and white youths respond to their desperate living conditions with violence and destruction.

1983

The Labour Party wins control of the city council, led by members of the Trotskyist Militant Tendency.

1984

Reopening of the Albert Dock, the visiting Tall Ships Race and the first International Garden Festival offer hope to Liverpool at a low point in its history.

1985–1990

Higson's is bought by Manchester brewer Boddington's. It is later taken over by Whitbread.

1988

Opening of Tate Liverpool, re-establishing Liverpool as a centre for contemporary art.

1990–

1990

Higson's ceases brewing at the Mersey Brewery. The brewery is sold to the GB Breweries.

1991

March. The Cain's brand is relaunched with the release of Cain's Traditional Bitter. GB Breweries is taken over by Danish brewing company, Bryggerigruppen A/S.

1993

Liverpool's dubious distinction as one of the poorest areas in the EU is recognised when the city receives Objective One status. Over the next decade this proves crucial in the city's regeneration.

1999

The first Liverpool Biennial of Contemporary Art.

2001

Summer. In the face of mounting losses brewing is stopped and the Danish parent company puts Robert Cain's brewery up for sale.

2002

The brewery is bought by Ajmail and Sudarghara Dusanj, who immediately restart production and begin rebuilding the brand.

2003

Liverpool celebrates the success of its bid to become European Capital of Culture, 2008. Cain's becomes the official beer.

2004

Cain's begins production of Cain's Finest Lager, the breakthrough product for the revived brewery and the first-ever British premium lager. The following year it is voted 'the greatest bottled lager' by GQ magazine.

2006

Cain's becomes the official beer of the Tate art galleries in Liverpool, London and St Ives.

2007

The Dusanj brothers merge Cain's with Honeycombe Leisure and take control of the new company, which now has well over 100 pubs and is known as the Cains Beer Company. In doing so Cain's is listed on the London stock exchange for the first time.

August. Liverpool celebrates its 800th anniversary year.

2008

Liverpool is European Capital of Culture.

February. Newcastle-based bank Northern Rock is nationalised, signalling the start of a global banking crisis.

Spring. Commodity and fuel prices rise sharply. Pubs suffer from falling sales.

July. Cains Beer Company annual report records half-yearly losses of £4.5 million. The Inland Revenue issues a 'winding-up order' over a tax dispute and Bank of Scotland refuses to renew the company's credit facility.

Liverpool enjoys a summer of spectacular art and cultural events.

7 August. Cains Beer Company goes into administration. Administrators quickly begin closing down pubs.

September. Dusanj brothers buy back the brewery and city centre pubs.

Bibliography

PRIMARY SOURCES

William Blackburn's brewer's ledger, 1862–1875, privately owned unpublished document

Liverpool census and other records, including Robert Cain's will

Company Reports of Higson's Brewery 1955–1984, Liverpool Records Office

Minutes of Robert Cain and Sons, 1897–1920, Liverpool Records Office

BOOKS AND ARTICLES

Belchem, John (ed.), *Liverpool 800: Culture, Character and History* (Liverpool: Liverpool University Press, 2006)

Belchem, John, and Donald M. MacRaild, 'Cosmopolitan Liverpool', in John Belchem (ed.), *Liverpool 800: Culture, Character and History* (Liverpool: Liverpool University Press, 2006), pp. 311–91

Belchem, John, *Merseypride: Essays in Liverpool Exceptionalism* (Liverpool: Liverpool University Press, 2nd edn, 2006)

'Cholera in Liverpool', *The Liverpool Mercury*, 30 January 1849

Cook, Norman, *Higson's Brewery, 1780–1980* (Liverpool: Kershaw Press Services, 1980)

'Death of a Liverpool Brewer', *The Liverpool Courier*, 20 July 1907

'Death of Mr. Robert Cain', *Daily Post and Mercury*, 20 July 1907

Duncan, W.H., *The Physical Causes of the High Rate of Mortality in Liverpool*, 1843

Engels, Frederick, *The Condition of the Working-Class in England in 1844*. With a Preface Written in 1892 (London: George Allen and Unwin, 1943)

Frazer, W.M., *Duncan of Liverpool* (Hamish Hamilton, 1947; repr. Preston: Carnegie Publishing, 1997)

'Funeral of Mr. Robert Cain', *Liverpool Courier*, 23 July 1907

'Funeral of Mr. Robert Cain', *Liverpool Daily Post*, 23 July 1907

'Funeral of Mr. Robert Cain', *The Liverpool Echo*, 22 July 1907

'Funeral: Sir William Cain', *The Times*, 9 May 1924

Gourvish, T.R., and R.G. Wilson, with research by Fiona Wood, *The British Brewing Industry, 1830–1980* (Cambridge: Cambridge University Press, 1994)

Grant, Linda, 'History broke Liverpool, and it broke my heart', *The Guardian*, 5 June 2003

Gutzke, David W., *Protecting the Pub: Brewers and Publicans Against Temperance* (Woodbridge: Royal Historical Society, Boydell Press, 1989)

Hawkins, K.H., and C.L. Pass, *The Brewing Industry: A Study in Industrial Organisation and Public Policy* (London: Heinemann, 1979)

Hawthorne, Nathaniel, *Passages from the English Notebooks of Nathaniel Hawthorne* (Boston: Houghton Mifflin, 1883)

Henri, Adrian, 'Poem for Liverpool 8', in Adrian Henri, Brian Patten and Roger McGough, *New Volume* (Harmondsworth: Penguin, 1983), p. 41

'Higson's Brewery Ltd.', *Illustrated Liverpool News*, September 1965, pp. 12–13

'House for Convalescent Officers: Sir. W. Cain's Gift', *The Times*, 18 October 1918

'I Dived the Cain's Mystery Lake', *Mersey Ale*, Spring 2005, p. 32

Jackson, Michael, 'Reincarnation of the Real Brewers', *The Independent*, 6 July 1991

Kennedy, David, and Michael Collins, 'Community Politics in Liverpool and the Governance of Professional Football in the Late Nineteenth Century', *The Historical Journal*, 49.3 (2006), pp. 761–88

Lane, Tony, *Liverpool: Gateway of Empire* (London: Lawrence and Wishart, 1987)

'Life of Robert Cain, The Large Local Brewer', *The Liverpool Review*, 17 September 1887, p. 10. Lithograph portrait of Cain on p. 1.

'Lord Brocket' (obituary), *The Times*, 22 November 1934

Macilwee, Michael, *The Gangs of Liverpool: From the Cornermen to the High Rip, the Mobs that Terrorised a City* (Wrea Green: Milo Books, 2006)

Malcolm, Tim, *Anti-Booze Crusaders in Victorian Liverpool* (Birkenhead: Countyvise, 2005)

Matthew, H.C.G., 'The Liberal Age, 1851–1914', in Kenneth O. Morgan (ed.), *The Oxford History of Britain* (Oxford: Oxford University Press, 2001), pp. 518–81

McGough, Roger, *Said and Done* (London: Century, 2005)

Melville, Herman, *Redburn* (1849; Harmondsworth: Penguin, 1986)

Milne, Graeme J., 'Maritime Liverpool', in John Belchem (ed.), *Liverpool 800: Culture, Character and History* (Liverpool: Liverpool University Press, 2006), pp. 257–309

Milne, Graeme J., *Trade and Traders in Mid-Victorian Liverpool: Mercantile Business and the Making of a World Port* (Liverpool: Liverpool University Press, 2000)

Monkton, H.A., *A History of English Ale and Beer* (London: The Bodley Head, 1966)

Morgan, Kenneth O. (ed.), *The Oxford History of Britain* (Oxford: Oxford University Press, 2001)

Murden, Jon, 'City of Change and Challenge: Liverpool since 1945', in John Belchem (ed.), *Liverpool 800: Culture, Character and History* (Liverpool: Liverpool University Press, 2006), pp. 393–485.

'News in Brief' (William Cain offers 'Wilton Grange' to the nation), *The Times*, 6 March 1916

Ó Tuathaigh, Gearóid, *Ireland Before the Famine, 1798–1848* (Dublin: Gill and Macmillan, 1972)

O'Connor, Freddy, *A Pub on Every Corner, Volume One: The City Centre* (Liverpool: Bluecoat Press, 1995)

Perrett, Brian, *Liverpool: A City at War* (Burscough: Hugo Press, 1990)

'Peter Walker (Warrington) and Robert Cain and Sons, Ltd' (share prospectus), *The Times*, 3 October 1921

'Peter Walker and Son, Warrington and Burton Ltd. A Successful Amalgamation', *The Times*, 31 March 1922

Pooley, Colin G., 'Living in Liverpool: The Modern City', in John Belchem (ed.), *Liverpool 800: Culture, Character and History* (Liverpool: Liverpool University Press, 2006), pp. 171–255.

Pratt, Edwin A., *The Licensed Trade: An Independent Survey* (London: John Murray, 1907)

'The Reappearance of the Shenandoah in British Waters', *The Times*, 8 November 1865

'The Rivington Project Suspended at Last', *The Liverpool Mercury*, 12 January 1849

Scally, Robert James, *The End of Hidden Ireland* (Oxford: Oxford University Press, 1995)

Sharples, Joseph, *Liverpool* (Pevsner Architectural Guides) (New Haven and London: Yale University Press, 2004)

Sharples, Joseph, *Merchant Palaces: Liverpool and Wirral Mansions Photographed by Bedford Lemere and Co.* (Liverpool: Bluecoat Press, 2007)

'Sir William Cain' (obituary), *The Times*, 7 May 1924

White, Brian D., *A History of the Corporation of Liverpool* (Liverpool: Liverpool University Press, 1951)

Wigney, George Adolphus, *A Theoretical and Practical Treatise on Malting and Brewing*, published by the author, 1895

Wilson, Paul, 'Mystery Lake Below Cain's Brewery Update', *Mersey Ale*, Winter 2004, p. 14

Winder, Robert, *Bloody Foreigners: The Story of Immigration to Britain* (London: Abacus, 2005)

Index

Printed and bound by CPI Group (UK) Ltd, Croydon, CR0 4YY

09/06/2025

14685812-0001